# Chinese and Wok Cooking

STEP-BY-STEP

# Chinese and Wok Cooking

## Shirley Gill

Photographs by Amanda Heywood

ACROPOLIS BOOKS

First published in 1996 by Lorenz Books

© 1996 Anness Publishing Limited

Lorenz Books is an imprint of
Anness Publishing Limited
Boundary Row Studios
1 Boundary Row
London SE1 8HP

Distributed in Canada by Raincoast Books Distribution Company

ISBN 1 85967 249 3

A CIP catalogue record is available from the British Library.

Publisher: Joanna Lorenz
Project Editor: Joanne Rippin
Home Economist: Nicola Fowler
Designer: Adrian Morris
Photographer: Amanda Heywood

MEASUREMENTS
Three sets of equivalent measurements have been provided in the recipes here, in the following
order: Metric, Imperial and American. It is essential that units of measurement are not mixed
within each recipe. Where conversions result in awkward numbers, these have been rounded for
convenience, but are still accurate enough to produce successful results.

Printed and bound in Hong Kong

# CONTENTS

# INTRODUCTION

Chinese cooking with a wok is light, fresh, fast and delicious – and easy too, be it stir-frying, steaming or deep frying. In this book you will find an exciting collection of fifty recipes inspired by the wealth of exotic ingredients imported from all corners of the eastern world – from Japan, India and South-east Asia as well as China. There are mouth-watering stir-fries, sensational soups and salads, tasty noodle dishes and spicy curries, all beautifully illustrated in colour with step-by-step instructions.

The sections on ingredients, techniques and equipment are brimming with advice and will arm you with the know-how to make the most of your wok. The ingredients used throughout the book are generally available from large supermarkets and oriental grocers. Don't be put off by any of the more unusual ingredients – these add an authentic note to the recipes and in many cases a unique flavour and aroma. Because cooking times are short, the emphasis is on quality and freshness. Cuts of meat should be lean and tender and vegetables and herbs bright and fresh.

I hope that the recipes which follow will give you an insight into the wok's versatility and that you too become devoted to this method of cooking, leaving your saucepans and frying pans on the kitchen shelf!

# Herbs, Spices and Flavourings

**Basil**
Several different types of basil are used in Asian cooking. Thai cooks use two varieties, holy and sweet basil, but ordinary basil works well in the recipes in this book.

**Cardamom**
Available both as tiny green pods and large black pods containing seeds, cardamom has a strong aromatic quality. For the recipes in this book, use the green ones either whole and lightly crushed or, if you want a more intense flavour, remove the seeds and discard the pods.

**Cashew Nuts**
Whole cashew nuts feature prominently in Chinese stir-fries, especially those with chicken.

**Chillies**
There is a wide range of fresh and dried chillies from which to choose. Generally the larger the chilli, the milder the flavour, but there are some exceptions, and the only way to gauge potency is by taste. Remove the seeds for a milder flavour. Whether using dried or fresh chillies, take care when preparing them as their seeds and flesh can "burn".

**Chilli Oil**
A red flavouring oil, sometimes containing chilli flakes. Use this oil sparingly.

**Chinese Five-spice Powder**
A distinctive Chinese flavouring containing star anise, pepper, fennel, cloves and cinnamon.

**Chinese Rice Vinegar**
Chinese white rice vinegar can sometimes be difficult to find outside Chinese supermarkets. If you cannot find it, use cider vinegar instead.

**Chinese Rice Wine**
Shaohsing wine is reputedly the finest variety. It has a rich sherry-like flavour and can be found in most larger supermarkets and oriental grocers.

**Coconut**
Coconut milk is used extensively in wok cookery, particularly in Thai curries. It can be freshly made or bought in cans, or you can use powdered or creamed coconut sold in blocks, and reconstitute them with water. Dried grated coconut flakes are available from good healthfood shops and make an excellent and interesting garnish.

**Coriander**
Widely used in wok cookery, it is also known as Chinese parsley. If the leaves are torn rather than chopped, the flavour is more subtle. Ground coriander tastes completely different from the fresh herb: it has a fairly mild, slightly musky flavour.

**Cumin**
Cumin has a strong, slightly bitter flavour and is used to flavour many Asian dishes.

**Dried Shrimps and Dried Shrimp Paste**
Dried shrimps are tiny shrimps that are salted and dried. They are used as a seasoning for stir-fried dishes. Soak them first in warm water until soft, then either process them in a blender or food processor or pound them in a mortar with a pestle. Shrimp paste is a dark odorous paste made from fermented shrimps. Use sparingly.

**Galangal**
Fresh galangal tastes and looks a little like ginger with a pinkish tinge to its skin, but is less pungent and more aromatic. It is also available dried and ground.

**Garlic**
One of the most indispensable ingredients in wok cookery for adding flavour. It can also be sliced and stir-fried to scatter over dishes as a garnish.

**Ginger**
Ginger has a sharp distinctive taste. Choose firm plump pieces with unwrinkled shiny skins.

**Groundnut Oil**
Also known as peanut oil, this has a mild nutty flavour. Its ability to be heated to a high temperature makes it perfect for stir-frying and deep frying.

**Hoisin Sauce**
This is a thick, dark brownish-red sauce which is sweet and spicy.

**Kaffir Lime Leaves**
Used like bay leaves, but to give an aromatic lime flavour to dishes. The fresh leaves are available from oriental shops and can be frozen for future use.

**Lemon Grass**
Lemon grass imparts a mild, sour-sweet, citrus flavour. Split and use whole or use finely chopped or ground to a paste.

**Mirin**
A mild, Japanese, sweet, rice cooking wine.

**Oyster Sauce**
A salty brown sauce made from boiled oysters and soy sauce.

**Peanuts**
Used in wok cookery to add flavour and a crunchy texture. The thin red skins of raw peanuts need to be removed first. To do this, simply immerse them in boiling water for a few minutes, after which you can easily slip off the skins.

**Sake**
A strong, powerful, fortified, rice wine from Japan.

**Salted Black Beans**
These salted fermented soy beans are available in cans and packets. Soak before use and check before seasoning a dish because of their salty nature.

**Sesame Oil**
This is made from toasted sesame seeds. It is very aromatic and is often added to a finished dish in small quantities.

**Soy Sauce**
A major seasoning ingredient in Asian cooking, this is made from fermented soy beans combined with yeast, salt and sugar. Chinese soy sauce falls into two main categories: light and dark. Japanese soy sauce (*shoyu*) has a slightly sweet and delicate flavour, while in Malaysian cooking *ketjap manis* is used – a sweet soy sauce with a more syrupy texture.

**Sweet Chilli Sauce**
A hot, yet sweet sauce made from chillies, vinegar, sugar and salt. Use sparingly in cooking, and also as a dipping sauce.

**Szechuan Peppercorns**
Red aromatic peppercorns which are best used roasted and ground.

**Tamarind**
The brown sticky pulp of the bean-like seed pod of the tamarind tree. The pulp is usually diluted with water and strained before use.

**Thai Fish Sauce**
Called *nam pla* in Thailand, this is used rather like soy sauce.

Top shelf, left to right: *garlic, ginger, lemon grass, dried shrimp, Thai fish sauce, Szechuan peppercorns, sweet chilli sauce, ground coriander, galangal, chinese five-spice powder, green chillies*

Middle shelf, left to right: *dried red chillies, peanuts (skin on), cardamom pods, cashew nuts (in jar), peanuts (skin off), kaffir lime leaves, tamarind, hoisin sauce, salted black beans, chilli oil*

Bottom shelf, back row: *sake, Chinese rice vinegar, Chinese rice wine*

Bottom shelf, middle row: *sesame oil, mirin, groundnut oil, coriander, cumin seeds*

Bottom shelf, front: *basil, dried shrimp paste, red & green chillies, flaked coconut & creamed coconut, light soy sauce, oyster sauce, pieces of coconut, whole coconut*

# Vegetables and Storecupboard Ingredients

Most of the vegetables used in this book will be familiar to you, but descriptions of some of the more exotic ones are given below for those who are more adventurous. Remember always to buy the best and freshest vegetables and cook them for only a short time so that they retain their crispness, colour and nutrients.

**Baby Sweetcorn**
Little young corn cobs have a crunchy texture and a mild, sweet flavour. Buy cobs with a bright yellow colour with no brown markings. They are widely available from supermarkets and oriental grocers.

**Bamboo Shoots**
These mild-flavoured tender shoots of the young bamboo are widely available fresh or sliced and halved in cans. Clean thoroughly before use.

**Beansprouts**
These shoots of the mung bean are usually available from supermarkets. They add a crisp texture to stir-fries.

**Chinese Cabbage**
Also known as Chinese leaves. It looks like a large, tightly packed cos lettuce with firm, pale green, crinkled leaves. It has a delicious crunchy texture.

**Chinese Pancakes**
These are flour-and-water pancakes with no seasonings or spices added. They are available fresh or frozen; if using frozen pancakes, thaw them thoroughly before steaming them.

**Gram Flour**
Gram flour is made from ground chick-peas and has a unique flavour. It is well worth seeking out in Indian food stores or healthfood shops, but you can use plain wholemeal flour instead, adding extra water.

**Mange-touts**
These tender green peapods containing flat, barely formed peas are highly valued for their crisp texture and sweet subtle flavour.

**Mushrooms**
Both fresh and dried mushrooms can be used in wok cookery to add texture and flavour to a dish. Dried mushrooms need to be soaked in warm water for 20–30 minutes before use. The soaking liquor can be used as a stock. Although dried mushrooms are expensive per pack, only a few are needed per recipe and they store indefinitely.

**Noodles**
An almost bewildering variety of fresh and dried noodles is available which can be interchanged in most recipes. Some need quick cooking; others need soaking in boiling water. They can be made from wheat, rice, ground beans or buckwheat. Follow the cooking instructions on the packet.

**Pak Choi**
An attractive vegetable with a long, smooth, milky-white stem and large, dark green leaves.

**Rice**
For the purposes of this book long grain white rice is used, varying from Thai jasmine to Indian basmati. Long grain rices such as patna and basmati tend to be drier and with the grains separate when cooked; Thai jasmine rice, although delicious, is soft, light and slightly stickier. Directions for cooking rice will be found in individual recipes.

**Shallots**
Shallots are small mild-flavoured members of the onion family with copper-red skins. They can be used in the same way as onions or ground into Thai curry pastes or fried into crisp flakes to be used as a garnish.

**Spring Onions**
The long slender spring onion is the immature bulb of the yellow onion. When recipes in this book refer to the "white" part it is to the firm, essentially white section which makes up most of the onion; "green" is the leaves.

**Spring Roll Wrappers**
Paper-thin wrappers made from wheat flour or rice flour and water. They are available in various sizes from most oriental grocers. Wheat flour wrappers are sold frozen and need to be thawed and carefully separated before use. Rice wrappers are dry and must be gently soaked before use.

**Tofu**
Tofu is also known as bean curd. Blocks of firm tofu are used in the recipes in this book as it is more suitable for stir-frying and deep frying. Although rather bland in flavour, it readily absorbs the flavours of the foods with which it is cooked. Tofu can be stored in the fridge for several days covered with water.

**Water Chestnuts**
A walnut-sized bulb of an Asian water plant that resembles a chestnut with its outer brown layer. Once peeled, the flesh is crisp and sweet. They are sold fresh by some oriental grocers, but are more readily available canned, whole or sliced.

**Wonton Wrappers**
Paper-thin squares of yellow-coloured dough, these are sold in most oriental food stores.

**Yard-long Beans**
These are long thin beans similar to French beans but three or four times longer. Cut into smaller lengths and use just like ordinary green beans.

Top shelf, left to right: *egg noodles, wonton wrappers, water chestnuts, cellophane noodles, gram flour, spring roll wrappers*

Middle shelf, left to right: *dried Chinese mushrooms, pak choi, tofu, egg noodles, Chinese pancakes*

Bottom, left to right: *rice, (in basket) mange-touts, baby sweetcorn, shallots, shiitake mushrooms, bamboo shoots, beansprouts, Chinese cabbage, spring onions, yard-long beans*

At front: *wood ears (mushrooms)*

# Equipment

**The equipment required for cooking the recipes in this book is generally simple and inexpensive, especially if you seek out authentic implements from oriental stores.**

### Balti Pan
Most Balti recipes are very simple to prepare and need very little equipment. In fact a lot of dishes are cooked and served in one pan called a karahi. This is to Balti cooking what the wok is to Chinese cooking. It is a round-based pan with two handles used for stir frying, braising and deep frying.

The balti pan is not essential for the recipes in this book: a wok or frying pan can be used instead, although the latter lacks the authenticity which is part of the fun of Balti cooking.

The wok has a number of accessories which work just as well with the karahi – a wok stand helps to keep it steady during deep frying, a wok scoop/spatula is shaped to fit the curves of the pan and a well-fitting domed lid can be used when braising. Like the wok a new karahi needs to be seasoned and allowed to take on the blackened patina that builds up over time, and which is said to improve the flavour of the food being cooked. Karahis can be bought at oriental supermarkets.

### Bamboo Steamer
For steaming this fits inside the wok, where it should rest safely perched on the sloping sides. It comes in various sizes, from small for dim sum to those large enough to hold a whole fish.

### Bamboo Strainer
A wide, flat, metal strainer with a long bamboo handle which makes lifting of foods from steam or hot oil easier. A metal slotted spoon can be used instead.

### Chopsticks
Long wooden chopsticks are useful for stirring, fluffing up rice, separating noodles during cooking and turning and transferring items.

### Cleaver
This all-purpose cutting tool is available in various weights and sizes. It is easy to use and serves many purposes from chopping up bones to precision cutting, like deveining prawns.

### Grater
Chinese graters are typically wooden.

### The Wok
Many varieties of wok are available, and while the term wok applies specifically to a Chinese cooking vessel, most Asian cooks use a version of this pan. The wok and its cousins are bowl-shaped with gently sloping sides which allow the heat to spread rapidly and evenly over the surface, thus making for rapid cooking which is fundamental to stir frying. The wok's large capacity also makes it excellent for deep frying, steaming and braising, although

care must be taken to keep it steady during these operations. The available woks may have an ear-shaped handle of metal or wood, a single long handle or both for you to choose from.

### Choosing a Wok
Choose a wok about 35 cm/14 in in diameter with good deep sides – this will be large enough for most recipes but not so large as to be unwieldly. Select one which is heavy and, if possible, made of carbon steel rather than stainless steel which tends to scorch. Cast iron is excellent too, as it is a good conductor of heat. Both metals develop a "non-stick" patina with use. Woks already lined with non-stick finishes are not advisable; not only are they more expensive but they cannot be seasoned like an ordinary wok nor can they withstand the high heat required for wok cooking. A traditional round-based wok works well on a gas hob, but flat-based woks are now available for use on electric hobs.

### Seasoning a Wok
All new woks except non-stick ones need to be seasoned. Many need to be scrubbed first with a cream cleanser to remove the manufacturer's protective coating of oil. Once the oil has been removed, place the wok over a low heat and add about 30 ml/2 tbsp vegetable oil. Using a pad of kitchen paper, rub the entire inside of the wok with the oil. Heat the wok slowly for 10–15 minutes and then wipe off the oil with more kitchen paper; the paper will become black. Repeat this process of coating, heating and wiping several times until the paper is clean.

The wok is now seasoned; do not scrub it again. After use, just

wash it in hot water without detergent, then wipe it dry. The wok will rust if not in constant use. If it does, scour the rust off and repeat the seasoning process.

### Wok Accessories
There is a range of accessories available to go with woks, although in most cases an adequate substitute may be found in the kitchen.

### Wok Brush
This bundle of stiff split bamboo is used for cleaning the wok. It is not essential and any ordinary kitchen brush will do just as well.

### Wok Lid
A wok lid is a dome-like cover, usually made of aluminium, which is used for steaming and braising. It may come with the wok or be purchased separately, but any domed saucepan lid which fits snugly over the top of the wok can be used instead.

### Wok Scoop/Spatula
A long-handled metal spatula with a wooden end used to toss and turn ingredients when stir-frying. Any good long-handled spoon can be used instead, although it does not have quite the same action.

### Wok Stand
Used to provide a secure base for the wok when it is used for steaming, braising or deep frying. Stands are made of metal and are either simple open-sided frames or solid metal rings with holes punched around the sides.

### Trivet
If you use your wok to steam, you will need a wooden or metal trivet to stand above the water level and support the plate.

bamboo steamer

wok brush

wooden
spatula

chopsticks

trivet

wok scoop

metal spatula

grater

strainer

wok stand and trivet

cleaver

wok

balti pan

# Preparing Ingredients

While stir-frying is quick and easy, it is essential to know how to prepare ingredients for cooking in order to be successful. Oriental cooks always use a cleaver for these tasks, but a sharp heavy knife can be used instead. For the ingredients to cook as quickly as possible and absorb the taste of the oil and flavourings despite the short cooking time, they should be cut into small uniform pieces and as many cut surfaces as possible should be exposed to the heat. Another reason for careful cutting is to enhance the visual appeal of a dish. This is why most oriental cuisines are so specific about cutting techniques, particularly vegetables.

## COOK'S TIP
Because ingredients are cooked for the minimum amount of time in a wok, use only the freshest of vegetables and only premium cuts of meat and poultry bought the same day.

## VEGETABLES
Some vegetables such as broccoli and cauliflower are cut according to their natural shape into florets; others are sliced, diagonally sliced, shredded, diced or roll cut depending on the dish.

## MEAT
Meat for stir-frying and sometimes steaming is cut into thin slices, matchstick strips or cubes. This way it can be quickly stir-fried or steamed without losing any of its tenderness.

**1** Diagonal cutting is a technique used for cutting vegetables such as carrots, asparagus or spring onions. It allows more of the surface of the vegetable to be exposed for quicker cooking. Simply angle the cleaver or knife at a slant and cut.

**2** Roll cutting is like diagonal cutting but is used for larger vegetables such as courgettes, aubergines or large carrots. Start by making one diagonal slice at one end of the vegetable, then turn it 180° and make the next diagonal cut. Continue until you have cut the entire vegetable into even-size chunks.

**1** Beef is always cut across the grain otherwise it would become tough; pork, lamb and chicken can be cut either along or across the grain.

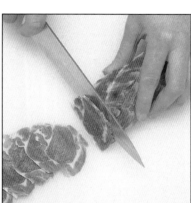

**2** Placing the meat in the freezer for about 1 hour beforehand makes it easier to cut paper-thin slices.

## CHOPPING HERBS

**1** Strip the leaves from the stalks and pile them on a chopping board.

**2** Using a cleaver or chef's knife, cut the herbs into small pieces, moving the blade back and forth until the herbs are as coarse or fine as you wish.

## PEELING AND CHOPPING LEMON GRASS

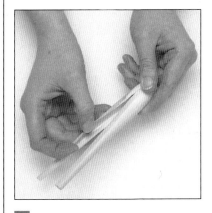 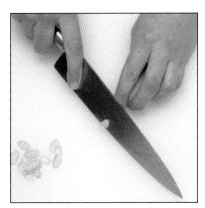

**1** Cut off and discard the dry leafy tops, leaving about 15 cm/6 in of stalk. Peel away any tough outer layers from the lemon grass.

**2** Lay the lemon grass on a board. Set a cleaver or chef's knife on top and strike it firmly with your fist – this helps to extract maximum flavour. Cut across the lemon grass to make thin slices, then continue chopping until fine.

## PREPARING BEANSPROUTS

**1** Pick over the beansprouts, discarding any that are discoloured, broken or wilted.

**2** Rinse the beansprouts under cold running water and drain well.

## PREPARING KAFFIR LIME LEAVES

**1** Using a small sharp knife, remove the centre vein.

**2** Cut the leaves crossways into very fine strips.

## PEELING AND CHOPPING GARLIC

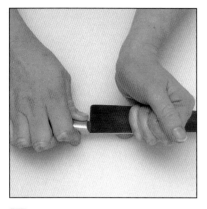

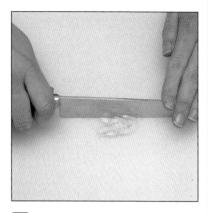

**1** Lay the unpeeled garlic clove on a board. Set the flat side of a cleaver or chef's knife on top and strike it firmly with your fist.

**2** Peel off and discard the skin. Finely chop the garlic, using the cleaver, moving the blade back and forth.

## CUTTING AND SHREDDING GARLIC AND GINGER

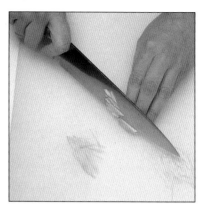

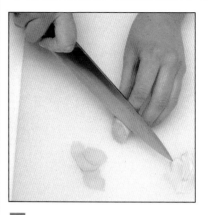

**1** Peel the skin from the root ginger or garlic clove. Using a cleaver or chef's knife, cut into thin slices.

**2** To cut into shreds, arrange the slices one on top of another and cut lengthways into fine strips.

## PEELING AND CHOPPING GINGER

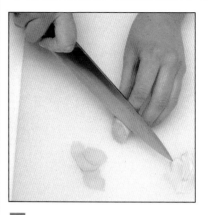

**1** Using a small sharp knife, peel the skin from the root ginger.

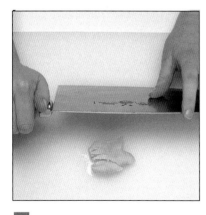

**2** Place the ginger on a board. Set the flat side of a cleaver or chef's knife on top and strike it firmly with your fist – this will soften its fibrous texture.

**3** Chop the ginger as coarsely or finely as you wish, moving the blade backwards and forwards.

## REMOVING SEEDS FROM CHILLIES

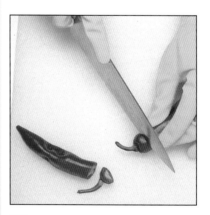

**1** Wearing rubber gloves, remove the stalks from chillies.

**2** Cut in half lengthways.

**3** Using a small sharp knife, scrape out the seeds and fleshy white ribs from each half.

# Garnishes

Many Asian dishes rely on garnishes to add a colourful finishing decorative touch. The garnishes can be simple, such as chopped coriander, fresh herb sprigs, or finely shredded spring onions or chilli, or more elaborate, such as cucumber fans, spring onion brushes and chilli flowers.

## CHILLI FLOWER

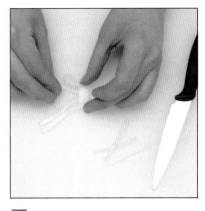

**1** Make several lengthways cuts through a chilli from below the stalk to the tip. Remove and discard any seeds.

**2** Soak the chilli in iced water until the ends curl to form a "flower". Pat dry with kitchen paper before use.

## CUCUMBER FAN

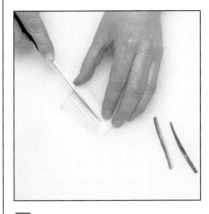

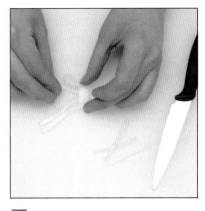

**1** Cut a slice of cucumber lengthways, about 7.5 cm/3 in long, avoiding the seeds. Remove any skin and cut into strips to within 1 cm/½ in from the end. Remove alternate strips.

**2** Carefully bend the strips towards the uncut end, tucking them in so that they stay securely in place. Leave to soak in iced water until required and pat dry before use.

## SPRING ONION BRUSH

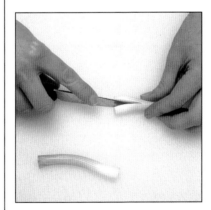

**1** Trim the green part of a spring onion and remove the base of the bulb – you should be left with a piece about 7.5 cm/3 in long. Make a lengthways cut about 2.5 cm/1 in long at one end of the spring onion.

**2** Roll the spring onion through 90° and cut again. Repeat this process at the other end. Place in iced water until the shreds open out and curl. Pat dry with kitchen paper before use.

# Spice Mixtures and Stocks

Use these spice mixtures to add heat and flavour to Thai curries, fish cakes and Balti dishes. They are quick and easy to make, but you can buy them ready-made from larger supermarkets.

## THAI RED CURRY PASTE

INGREDIENTS
4 fresh red chillies
2.5 cm/1 in piece fresh root
    ginger
4 shallots
4–6 garlic cloves
4 lemon grass stalks
20 ml/4 tsp coriander seeds
10 ml/2 tsp cumin seeds
20 ml/2 tsp hot paprika
1.5 ml/¼ tsp ground turmeric
2.5 ml/½ tsp salt
grated rind and juice of 2 limes
15 ml/1 tbsp vegetable oil

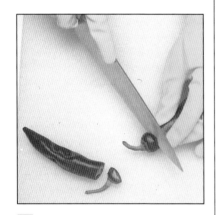

**1** Peel and chop the ginger, shallots and garlic. Peel and finely chop the lemon grass. Wearing rubber gloves, remove the stalks from the chillies, then cut them in half lengthways. Scrape out the seeds and fleshy white ribs, then roughly chop the flesh.

## THAI GREEN CURRY PASTE

INGREDIENTS
6 spring onions
4 fresh coriander stems, washed
4 kaffir lime leaves
6–8 fresh green chillies
4 garlic cloves, chopped
2.5 cm/1 in piece fresh root
    ginger, chopped
1 lemon grass stalk, chopped
45 ml/3 tbsp chopped fresh
    coriander
45 ml/3 tbsp chopped fresh basil
15 ml/1 tbsp vegetable oil

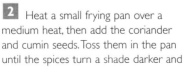

**2** Heat a small frying pan over a medium heat, then add the coriander and cumin seeds. Toss them in the pan until the spices turn a shade darker and emit a roasted aroma. Leave to cool.

**3** Place all the ingredients in a blender or food processor and process to form a smooth paste. Store in a screw-top jar for up to 1 month in the fridge and use as required.

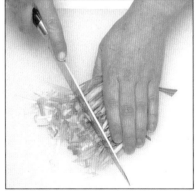

**1** Chop the spring onions and coriander stems. Remove the centre vein from the kaffir lime leaves, then cut into fine shreds. Seed and chop the chillies.

**2** Put all the ingredients in a blender or food processor and process to form a smooth paste. Store in a screw-top jar for up to 2 weeks in the fridge and use as required.

## GARAM MASALA

INGREDIENTS
7.5 cm/3 in piece cinnamon stick
2 bay leaves
5 ml/1 tsp cumin seeds
5 ml/1 tsp whole cloves
5 ml/1 tsp black peppercorns
¼ nutmeg, grated

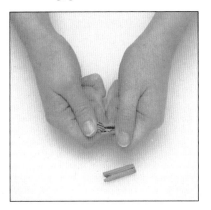

**1** Break the cinnamon stick into pieces. Crumble the bay leaves.

**2** Heat a small frying pan over a medium heat, then add the bay leaves and all the spices except the nutmeg. Dry-roast until the spices turn a shade darker and emit a roasted aroma, stirring or shaking the pan frequently to prevent burning. Leave to cool. Place all the ingredients in a spice mill or electric coffee grinder and grind to a fine powder. Store in a small jar with a tight-fitting lid for up to 2 months.

## CHICKEN STOCK

INGREDIENTS
1 kg/2¼ lb uncooked chicken
    bones, such as backs, wings etc.
500 g/1¼ lb chicken pieces
2.4 litres/4 pints/10 cups water
2 thin slices fresh root ginger
2 spring onions, white parts only
2 unpeeled garlic cloves
salt, to taste

**1** Place all the ingredients except the salt in a large pan and bring to a simmer. Skim off any scum. Simmer for 3–4 hours to extract all the flavour. Season with salt to taste.

**2** Strain the stock, pressing the solid ingredients with the back of a ladle or spoon to extract all the liquid. Allow the stock to cool, then chill. Spoon off the fat from the surface. Use as required.

## FRESH COCONUT MILK

INGREDIENTS
grated fresh coconut to fill a
    measuring jug to the 400 ml/
    14 fl oz/1⅔ cups mark
300ml/½ pint/1¼ cups hot
    water

**1** First you will need to break open a fresh coconut. To do this, push a skewer into the three holes in the top of the coconut and drain out the liquid. Place the coconut in a plastic bag and hit it hard with a hammer. To remove the outer shell from the coconut pieces, prise the tip of a small sharp knife between it and the coconut flesh. Remove the inner brown skin using a potato peeler. Grate the flesh.

**2** Put the measured grated coconut and hot water into a blender or food processor fitted with a metal blade and process for 1 minute. Strain the coconut mixture through a sieve lined with muslin into a bowl, gathering up the corners of the cloth and squeezing out the liquid. The coconut milk is now ready; stir before use.

left to right:
*chicken stock*
*garam masala*
*fresh coconut*
    *milk*

# Cooking Techniques

## STIR-FRYING

This quick technique retains the fresh flavour, colour and texture of ingredients and its success depends upon having all the required ingredients ready prepared before cooking.

**1** Heat an empty wok over a high heat. This prevents food sticking and will ensure an even heat. Add the oil and swirl it around so that it coats the base and halfway up the sides of the wok. It is important that the oil is hot enough so that when food is added it will start to cook immediately, but it should not be so hot that it is smoking.

**2** Ingredients should then be added in a specific order, usually aromatics first (garlic, ginger, spring onions). If this is the case, do not wait for the oil to get so hot that it is almost smoking or they will burn and become bitter. Toss them in the oil for a few seconds. Now add the main ingredients which require longer cooking, such as dense vegetables or meat, followed by the faster-cooking items. Toss and turn the ingredients from the centre of the wok to the sides.

## DEEP FRYING

A wok is ideal for deep frying as it uses far less oil than a deep-fat fryer. Make sure, however, that it is fully secure on its stand before adding the oil and never leave the wok unattended.

**1** Put the wok on a stand and half-fill with oil. Heat until the required temperature registers on a thermometer. Alternatively, test it by dropping in a small piece of food; if bubbles form all over the surface of the food, the oil is ready.

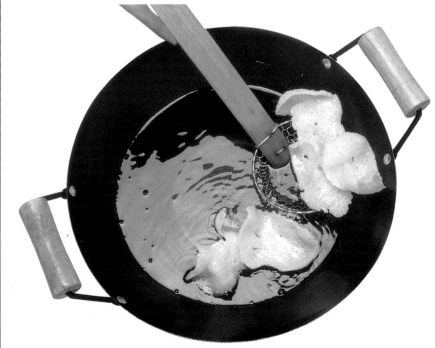

**2** Carefully add the food to the oil using long wooden chopsticks or tongs and move it around to prevent it sticking together. Using a bamboo strainer or slotted spoon, carefully remove the food and drain on kitchen paper before serving.

## STEAMING

Steamed foods are cooked by a gentle moist heat which must circulate freely in order for the food to cook. Increasingly popular with health conscious cooks, steaming preserves flavour and nutrients. It is perfect for vegetables, meat, poultry and especially fish. The easiest way to steam in a wok is with a bamboo steamer but you can do without.

### USING A BAMBOO STEAMER IN A WOK

**1** Put the wok on a stand. Pour about 5 cm/2 in water into the wok and bring to simmering point. Put the bamboo steamer containing the food into the wok, where it will rest on the sloping sides.

**2** Cover the steamer with its matching lid and steam for the recommended time. Check the water level occasionally and top up with boiling water as necessary.

### USING A WOK AS A STEAMER

**1** Place a trivet in the wok, then place the wok on its stand on the hob. Pour in enough boiling water to come just below the trivet, then carefully place the plate holding whatever is to be steamed on the trivet.

**2** Cover the wok with its lid, bring to the boil, then lower the heat to a gentle simmer. Steam for the recommended time, checking the water level occasionally and topping up with boiling water as necessary.

# Lettuce-wrapped Garlic Lamb

For this tasty starter lamb is stir-fried with garlic, ginger and spices, then served in crisp lettuce leaves with yogurt, a dab of lime pickle and mint leaves – the contrast of hot and spicy and cool and crisp is excellent.

## Serves 4

INGREDIENTS
450 g/1 lb lamb neck fillet
2.5 ml/½ tsp chilli powder
10 ml/2 tsp ground coriander
5 ml/1 tsp ground cumin
2.5 ml/½ tsp ground turmeric
30 ml/2 tbsp groundnut oil
3–4 garlic cloves, chopped
15 ml/1 tbsp grated fresh
   root ginger
150 ml/¼ pint/⅔ cup lamb
   stock or water
4–6 spring onions, sliced
30 ml/2 tbsp chopped
   fresh coriander
15 ml/1 tbsp lemon juice
lettuce leaves, yogurt, lime pickle
   and mint leaves, to serve

*coriander*

*stock*

*garlic*

*lamb*

*ginger*

*groundnut oil*

*spring onions*

VARIATION
Vegetables, such as cooked diced potatoes or peas, can be added to the mince.

**1** Trim the lamb fillet of any fat and cube in to small pieces, then mince in a blender or food processor, taking care not to over-process.

**2** In a bowl mix together the chilli powder, ground coriander, cumin and turmeric. Add the lamb and rub the spice mixture into the meat. Cover and leave to marinate for about 1 hour.

**3** Heat a wok until hot. Add the oil and swirl it around. When hot, add the garlic and ginger and allow to sizzle for a few seconds.

**4** Add the lamb and continue to stir-fry for 2–3 minutes.

**5** Pour in the stock and continue to stir-fry until all the stock has been absorbed and the lamb is tender, adding more stock if necessary.

**6** Add the spring onions, fresh coriander and lemon juice, then stir-fry for a further 30–45 seconds. Serve at once with the lettuce leaves, yogurt, pickle and mint leaves.

# Crispy "Seaweed" with Flaked Almonds

This popular starter in Chinese restaurants is in fact usually made not with seaweed but spring greens! It is easy to make at home and the result is delicious.

## Serves 4-6

INGREDIENTS
450 g/1 lb spring greens
groundnut oil, for deep-frying
1.5 ml/¼ tsp sea salt flakes
5 ml/1 tsp caster sugar
50 g/2 oz/½ cup flaked
almonds, toasted

*spring greens*

*almonds*

*groundnut oil*

*sea salt*

*sugar*

## COOK'S TIP
It is important to dry the spring greens thoroughly before deep-frying them, otherwise it will be difficult to achieve the desired crispness without destroying their vivid colour.

**1** Wash the spring greens under cold running water and pat well with kitchen paper to dry thoroughly. Remove and discard the thick white stalks from the spring greens.

**2** Lay several leaves on top of one another, roll up tightly and, using a sharp knife, slice as finely as possible into thread-like strips.

**3** Half-fill a wok with oil and heat to 180°C/350°F. Deep fry the spring greens in batches for about 1 minute until they darken and crisp. Remove each batch from the wok as soon as it is ready and drain on kitchen paper.

**4** Transfer the "seaweed" to a serving dish, sprinkle with the salt and sugar, then mix well. Garnish with the toasted flaked almonds scattered over.

# Thai Fish Cakes

Bursting with the flavours of chillies, lime and lemon grass, these little fish cakes make a wonderful starter.

*Serves 4*

INGREDIENTS

450 g/1 lb white fish fillets, such as cod or haddock
3 spring onions, sliced
30 ml/2 tbsp chopped fresh coriander
30 ml/2 tbsp Thai red curry paste
1 fresh green chilli, seeded and chopped
10 ml/2 tsp grated lime rind
15 ml/1 tbsp lime juice
30 ml/2 tbsp groundnut oil
salt, to taste
crisp lettuce leaves, shredded spring onions, fresh red chilli slices, coriander sprigs and lime wedges, to serve

*lettuce*          *white fish fillets*

*lime*        *spring onions*

*groundnut oil*

*coriander*

*red chilli*

*green chilli    Thai red curry paste*

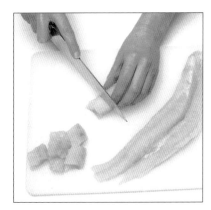

**1** Cut the fish into chunks, then place in a blender or food processor.

**2** Add the spring onions, coriander, red curry paste, green chilli, lime rind and juice to the fish. Season with salt. Process until finely minced.

**3** Using lightly floured hands, divide the mixture into 16 pieces and shape each one into a small cake about 4 cm/1½ in across. Place the fish cakes on a plate, cover with clear film and chill for about 2 hours until firm. Heat the wok over a high heat until hot. Add the oil and swirl it around.

**4** Fry the fish cakes, a few at a time, for 6–8 minutes, turning them carefully until evenly browned. Drain each batch on kitchen paper and keep hot while cooking the remainder. Serve on a bed of crisp lettuce leaves with shredded spring onions, red chilli slices, coriander sprigs and lime wedges.

# Chinese Spiced Salt Spareribs

Fragrant with spices, this authentic Chinese dish makes a great starter to an informal meal. Don't forget the finger bowls!

## *Serves 4*

INGREDIENTS
675-900 g/1½-2 lb meaty
    pork spareribs
25 ml/1½ tbsp cornflour
groundnut oil, for deep frying
coriander sprigs, to garnish

FOR THE SPICED SALT
5 ml/1 tsp Szechuan peppercorns
30 ml/2 tbsp coarse sea salt
2.5 ml/½ tsp Chinese five-
    spice powder

FOR THE MARINADE
30 ml/2 tbsp light soy sauce
5 ml/1 tsp caster sugar
15 ml/1 tbsp Chinese rice wine
ground black pepper

*Chinese rice wine*

*pork spareribs*

*Chinese five-spice powder*

*Szechuan peppercorns*

*coriander*

*light soy sauce*

*groundnut oil*

*sea salt*

**1** Using a heavy sharp cleaver, chop the spareribs into pieces about 5 cm/ 2 in long or ask your butcher to do this, then place them in a shallow dish.

**2** To make the spiced salt, heat a wok to a medium heat. Add the Szechuan peppercorns and salt and dry fry for about 3 minutes, stirring constantly until the mixture colours slightly. Remove from the heat and stir in the five-spice powder. Leave to cool.

**3** Using a mortar and pestle or an electric coffee grinder, grind the spiced salt to a fine powder.

**4** Sprinkle 5 ml/1 tsp of the spiced salt over the spareribs and rub in well with your hands. Add the soy sauce, sugar, rice wine or sherry and some freshly ground black pepper, then toss the ribs in the marinade until well coated. Cover and leave to marinate in the fridge for about 2 hours, turning the spareribs occasionally.

## COOK'S TIP
Any leftover spiced salt can be kept for several months in a screw-top jar. Use to rub on the flesh of duck, chicken or pork before cooking.

**5** Pour off any excess marinade from the spareribs. Sprinkle the pieces with cornflour and mix well to coat evenly.

**6** Half-fill a wok with oil and heat to 180°C/350°F. Deep fry the spareribs in batches for 3 minutes until pale golden. Remove and set aside. Reheat the oil to the same temperature. Return the spareribs to the oil and deep-fry for a second time for 1–2 minutes until crisp and thoroughly cooked. Drain on kitchen paper. Transfer the ribs to a warmed serving platter and sprinkle over 5–7.5 ml/1–1½ tsp spiced salt. Garnish with coriander sprigs.

# Steamed Spiced Pork and Water Chestnut Wontons

Ginger and Chinese five-spice powder flavour this version of steamed open dumplings – a favourite snack in many teahouses.

## Makes about 36

INGREDIENTS
2 large Chinese cabbage leaves, plus extra for lining the steamer
2 spring onions, finely chopped
1 cm/½ in piece fresh root ginger, finely chopped
50 g/2oz canned water chestnuts (drained weight), rinsed and finely chopped
225 g/8oz minced pork
2.5 ml/½ tsp Chinese five-spice powder
15 ml/1 tbsp cornflour
15 ml/1 tbsp light soy sauce
15 ml/1 tbsp Chinese rice wine
10 ml/2 tsp sesame oil
generous pinch of caster sugar
about 36 wonton wrappers, each 7.5 cm/3 in square
light soy sauce and hot chilli oil, for dipping

caster sugar

Chinese cabbage

spring onions

light soy sauce

sesame oil

cornflour

wonton wrappers

water chestnuts

pork

Chinese five-spice powder

Chinese rice wine

ginger

VARIATION
These can also be deep fried, in which case fold the edges over the filling to enclose it completely. Press well to seal. Deep fry in batches in hot oil for about 2 minutes.

**1** Place the Chinese cabbage leaves one on top of another. Cut them lengthways into quarters and then across into thin shreds.

**2** Place the shredded Chinese cabbage leaves in a bowl. Add the spring onions, ginger, water chestnuts, pork, five-spice powder, cornflour, soy sauce, rice wine, sesame oil and sugar; mix well.

**3** Set one wonton wrapper on a work surface. Place a heaped teaspoon of the filling in the centre of the wrapper, then lightly dampen the edges with water.

**4** Lift the wrapper up around the filling, gathering to form a purse. Squeeze the wrapper firmly around the middle, then tap on the bottom to make a flat base. The top should be open. Place the wonton on a tray and cover with a damp dish towel.

**5** Line the steamer with cabbage leaves and steam the dumplings for 12–15 minutes until tender. Remove each batch from the steamer as soon as they are cooked, cover with foil and keep warm. Serve hot with soy sauce and chilli oil for dipping.

# Vegetable Tempura

These deep-fried fritters are based on Kaki-age, a Japanese dish that often incorporates fish and prawns as well as vegetables.

## Makes 8

INGREDIENTS
2 medium courgettes
½ medium aubergine
1 large carrot
½ small Spanish onion
1 egg
120 ml/4 fl oz/½ cup
   iced water
115 g/4 oz/1 cup plain flour
salt and ground black pepper
vegetable oil, for deep-frying
sea salt flakes, lemon slices and
   Japanese soy sauce (*shoyu*),
   to serve

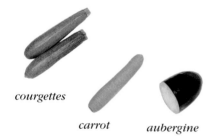

*courgettes*

*carrot*    *aubergine*

*Spanish onion*

*plain flour*

*egg*       *vegetable oil*

**COOK'S TIP**
Paring strips of peel from the courgettes and aubergine will avoid too much tough skin in the finished dish.

**1** Using a potato peeler, pare strips of peel from the courgettes and aubergine to give a stripy effect.

**2** Cut the courgettes, aubergine and carrot into strips about 7.5–10 cm/3–4 in long and 3 mm/⅛ in wide.

**3** Put the courgettes, aubergine and carrot in a colander and sprinkle liberally with salt. Leave for about 30 minutes, then rinse thoroughly under cold running water. Drain well.

**4** Thinly slice the onion from top to base, discarding the plump pieces in the middle. Separate the layers so that there are lots of fine long strips. Mix all the vegetables together and season with salt and pepper.

**5** Make the batter immediately before frying: mix the egg and iced water in a bowl, then sift in the flour. Mix very briefly using a fork or chopsticks. Do not overmix – the batter should remain lumpy. Add the vegetables to the batter and mix to combine.

**6** Meanwhile, half-fill a wok with oil and heat to 180°C/350°F. Scoop up one heaped tablespoon of the mixture at a time and carefully lower into the oil. Deep fry in batches for about 3 minutes until golden brown and crisp. Drain on kitchen paper. Serve each diner with salt, lemon slices and a tiny bowl of Japanese soy sauce for dipping.

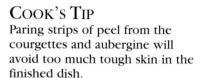

# Hot Spicy Crab Claws

Crab claws are used to delicious effect in this quick starter based on an Indonesian dish called *Kepiting Pedas*.

*Serves 4*

INGREDIENTS
12 fresh or frozen and thawed
    cooked crab claws
4 shallots, roughly chopped
2-4 fresh red chillies, seeded and
    roughly chopped
3 garlic cloves, roughly chopped
5 ml/1 tsp grated fresh
    root ginger
2.5 ml/½ tsp ground coriander
45 ml/3 tbsp groundnut oil
60 ml/4 tbsp water
10 ml/2 tsp sweet soy sauce
    (*kecap manis*)
10-15 ml/2-3 tsp lime juice
salt, to taste

*shallots*

*crab claws*

*sweet soy sauce*

*garlic*

*coriander*

*red chillies*        *groundnut oil*

*lime*        *ginger*

**1**  Crack the crab claws with the back of a heavy knife to make eating easier. Set aside. In a mortar, pound the chopped shallots with the pestle until pulpy. Add the chillies, garlic, ginger and ground coriander and pound until the mixture forms a coarse paste.

**2**  Heat the wok over a medium heat. Add the oil and swirl it around. When it is hot, stir in the chilli paste. Stir-fry for about 30 seconds. Increase the heat to high. Add the crab claws and stir-fry for another 3–4 minutes.

**3**  Stir in the water, sweet soy sauce, lime juice and salt to taste. Continue to stir-fry for 1–2 minutes. Serve at once, garnished with fresh coriander. The crab claws are eaten with the fingers, so provide finger bowls.

## COOK'S TIP
If whole crab claws are unavailable look out for frozen ready-prepared crab claws. These are shelled with just the tip of the claw attached to the white meat. Stir fry for about two minutes until hot through.

# Sweetcorn and Chicken Soup

This popular classic Chinese soup is delicious, and very easy to make.

*Serves 4-6*

INGREDIENTS

1 chicken breast fillet, about
    115 g/4 oz, cubed
10 ml/2 tsp light soy sauce
15 ml/1 tbsp Chinese rice wine
5 ml/1 tsp cornflour
60 ml/4 tbsp cold water
5 ml/1 tsp sesame oil
30 ml/2 tbsp groundnut oil
5 ml/1 tsp grated fresh root
    ginger
1 litre/1¾ pints/4 cups chicken
    stock
425 g/15 oz can cream-style
    sweetcorn
225 g/8 oz can sweetcorn kernels
2 eggs, beaten
2-3 spring onions, green parts
    only, cut into tiny rounds
salt and ground black pepper

*cornflour*

*chicken stock*

*cream-style sweetcorn*

*chicken*

*sweetcorn kernels*

*egg*

*sesame oil*

*ginger*

*Chinese rice wine*

**1** Mince the chicken in a food processor, taking care not to over-process. Transfer the chicken to a bowl and stir in the soy sauce, rice wine, cornflour, water, sesame oil and seasoning. Cover and leave for about 15 minutes to absorb the flavours.

**2** Heat a wok over a medium heat. Add the groundnut oil and swirl it around. Add the ginger and stir-fry for a few seconds. Add the stock, creamed sweetcorn and sweetcorn kernels. Bring to just below boiling point.

**3** Spoon about 90 ml/6 tbsp of the hot liquid into the chicken mixture until it forms a smooth paste and stir. Return to the wok. Slowly bring to the boil, stirring constantly, then simmer for 2–3 minutes until cooked.

**4** Pour the beaten eggs into the soup in a slow steady stream, using a fork or chopsticks to stir the top of the soup in a figure-of-eight pattern. The egg should set in lacy shreds. Serve immediately with the spring onions sprinkled over.

# Crispy Spring Rolls with Sweet Chilli Dipping Sauce

Miniature spring rolls make delicious starters or party finger food.

## *Makes 20-24*

INGREDIENTS
25 g/1 oz rice vermicelli noodles
groundnut oil
5 ml/1 tsp grated fresh
    root ginger
2 spring onions, finely shredded
50 g/2 oz carrot, finely shredded
50 g/2 oz mange-touts, shredded
25 g/1 oz young spinach leaves
50 g/2 oz fresh beansprouts
15 ml/1 tbsp chopped fresh mint
15 ml/1 tbsp chopped
    fresh coriander
30 ml/2 tbsp Thai fish sauce
    (*nam pla*)
20-24 spring roll wrappers, each
    13 cm/5 in square
1 egg white, lightly beaten

FOR THE DIPPING SAUCE
50 g/2 oz/4 tbsp caster sugar
50 ml/2 fl oz/¼ cup rice vinegar
2 fresh red chillies, seeded and
    finely chopped

*noodles*  *spinach*

*spring onions*

*spring roll wrappers*

*Thai fish sauce*

*mange-touts*

*beansprouts*  *ginger*  *carrot*

**1** First make the dipping sauce: place the sugar and vinegar in a small pan with 30 ml/2 tbsp water. Heat gently, stirring until the sugar dissolves, then boil rapidly until it forms a light syrup. Stir in the chillies and leave to cool.

**2** Soak the noodles according to the packet instructions; rinse and drain well. Using scissors, snip the noodles into short lengths.

**3** Heat a wok until hot. Add 15 ml/ 1 tbsp oil and swirl it around. Add the ginger and spring onions and stir-fry for 15 seconds. Add the carrot and mange-touts and stir-fry for 2–3 minutes. Add the spinach, beansprouts, mint, coriander, fish sauce and noodles and stir-fry for a further minute. Set aside to cool.

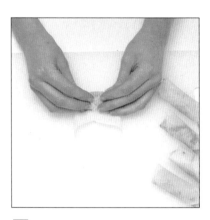

**4** Take one spring roll wrapper and arrange it so that it faces you in a diamond shape. Place a spoonful of filling just below the centre, then fold up the bottom point over the filling.

**6** Half-fill a wok with oil and heat to 180°C/350°F. Deep fry the spring rolls in batches for 3–4 minutes until golden and crisp. Drain on kitchen paper. Serve hot with the sweet chilli dipping sauce.

**5** Fold in each side, then roll up tightly. Brush the end with beaten egg white to seal. Repeat until all the filling has been used.

# Quick-fried Prawns with Hot Spices

These spicy prawns that cook in moments make a wonderful starter. Don't forget to provide your guests with finger bowls.

## Serves 4

INGREDIENTS

450 g/1 lb large raw prawns
2.5 cm/1 in piece fresh root
    ginger, grated
2 garlic cloves, crushed
5 ml/1 tsp hot chilli powder
5 ml/1 tsp ground turmeric
10 ml/2 tsp black mustard seeds
seeds from 4 green cardamom
    pods, crushed
50 g/2 oz/4 tbsp ghee or butter
120 ml/4fl oz/½ cup coconut milk
30–45 ml/2–3 tbsp chopped fresh
    coriander
salt and ground black pepper
naan bread, to serve

*prawns*

*coconut milk*

*coriander*

*chilli powder*

*ghee*

*black mustard seeds*

*turmeric*

*ginger*

*garlic*

*cardamom pods*

COOK'S TIP
If raw prawns are unavailable, use cooked ones instead, but simmer gently in the coconut milk for just 1-2 minutes.

**1** Peel the prawns carefully, leaving the tails attached.

**2** Using a small sharp knife, make a slit along the back of each prawn and remove the dark vein. Rinse under cold running water, drain and pat dry.

**3** Put the ginger, garlic, chilli powder, turmeric, mustard seeds and cardamom seeds in a bowl. Add the prawns and toss to coat with the spice mixture.

**4** Heat a karahi or wok until hot. Add the ghee or butter and swirl it around until foaming.

**5** Add the marinated prawns and stir-fry for 1–1½ minutes until they are just turning pink.

**6** Stir in the coconut milk and simmer for 3–4 minutes until the prawns are cooked through. Season with salt and pepper. Sprinkle over the coriander and serve at once with naan bread.

# Thai Seafood Salad

This seafood salad with chilli, lemon grass and fish sauce is light and refreshing.

*Serves 4*

INGREDIENTS
225 g/8 oz ready-prepared squid
225 g/8 oz raw tiger prawns
8 scallops, shelled
225 g/8 oz firm white fish
30-45 ml/2-3 tbsp olive oil
small mixed lettuce leaves and
    coriander sprigs, to serve

FOR THE DRESSING
2 small fresh red chillies, seeded
    and finely chopped
5 cm/2 in piece lemon grass,
    finely chopped
2 fresh kaffir lime leaves,
    shredded
30 ml/2 tbsp Thai fish sauce
    (*nam pla*)
2 shallots, thinly sliced
30 ml/2 tbsp lime juice
30 ml/2 tbsp rice vinegar
10 ml/2 tsp caster sugar

*white fish*          *squid*

*tiger prawns*
        *scallops*
                *lemon grass*

*Thai fish sauce*

*shallots*          *kaffir lime leaves*

**1** Prepare the seafood: slit open the squid bodies, score the flesh with a sharp knife, then cut into square pieces. Halve the tentacles, if necessary. Peel and devein the prawns. Remove the dark beard-like fringe and tough muscle from the scallops. Cube the white fish.

**2** Heat a wok until hot. Add the oil and swirl it around, then add the prawns and stir-fry for 2–3 minutes until pink. Transfer to a large bowl. Stir-fry the squid and scallops for 1–2 minutes until opaque. Remove and add to the prawns. Stir-fry the white fish for 2–3 minutes. Remove and add to the cooked seafood. Reserve any juices.

**3** Put all the dressing ingredients in a small bowl with the reserved juices from the wok; mix well.

**4** Pour the dressing over the seafood and toss gently. Arrange the salad leaves and coriander sprigs on four individual plates, then spoon the seafood on top. Serve at once.

# Spicy Battered Fish

These crispy, spicy fritters are based on a dish from Baltistan, India.

## Serves 4

### INGREDIENTS
10 ml/2 tsp cumin seeds
10 ml/2 tsp coriander seeds
1–2 dried red chillies
30 ml/2 tbsp vegetable oil
175 g/6 oz/1½ cups gram flour
5 ml/1 tsp salt
10 ml/2 tsp garam masala
about 250 ml/8 fl oz/1 cup water
groundnut oil, for deep-frying
675 g/1½ lb fish fillets, such as
  cod, skinned, boned and cut
  into thick strips
mint sprigs and lime halves,
  to garnish

*fish fillets*

*groundnut oil*

*red chillies*

*gram flour*

*vegetable oil*

*coriander*

*garam masala*

**1** Crush the cumin, coriander and chilli(es), using a pestle and mortar. Heat the vegetable oil in a karahi or wok and stir-fry the spices for 1–2 minutes.

**2** Put the gram flour, salt, spice mixture and garam masala in a bowl. Gradually stir in enough water to make a thick batter. Cover and leave to rest for 30 minutes.

**3** Half-fill a karahi or wok with groundnut oil and heat to 190°C/375°F. When the oil is ready, dip the fish, a few pieces at a time, into the batter, shaking off any excess.

**4** Deep fry the fish in batches for 4–5 minutes until golden brown. Drain on kitchen paper. Serve immediately, garnished with mint sprigs and lime halves for squeezing over.

# Fish Balls with Chinese Greens

These tasty fish balls are easy to make using a food processor. Here they are partnered with a selection of green vegetables – pak choi is available from oriental stores.

*Serves 4*

INGREDIENTS
FOR THE FISH BALLS
450 g/1 lb white fish fillets, skinned, boned and cubed
3 spring onions, chopped
1 back bacon rasher, rinded and chopped
15 ml/1 tbsp Chinese rice wine
30 ml/2 tbsp light soy sauce
1 egg white

FOR THE VEGETABLES
1 small head pak choi
5 ml/1 tsp cornflour
15 ml/1 tbsp light soy sauce
150 ml/¼ pint/⅔ cup fish stock
30 ml/2 tbsp groundnut oil
2 garlic cloves, sliced
2.5 cm/1 in piece fresh root ginger, cut into thin shreds
75 g/3 oz green beans
175 g/6 oz mange-touts
3 spring onions, sliced diagonally into 5–7.5cm/2–3 in lengths
salt and ground black pepper

*garlic*

*ginger*

*bacon*

*spring onions*

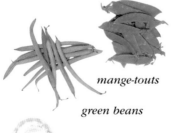

*mange-touts*

*green beans*

*light soy sauce*

*fish stock*

*pak choi*

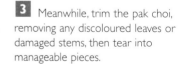

*fish fillets*

*Chinese rice wine*

*groundnut oil*

**1** Put the fish, spring onions, bacon, rice wine, soy sauce and egg white in a food processor. Process until smooth. With wetted hands, form the mixture into about 24 small balls.

**2** Steam the fish balls in batches in a lightly greased bamboo steamer in a wok for 5–10 minutes until firm. Remove from the steamer and keep warm.

**3** Meanwhile, trim the pak choi, removing any discoloured leaves or damaged stems, then tear into manageable pieces.

**4** In a small bowl blend together the cornflour, soy sauce and stock. Set aside.

## VARIATION
Replace the mange-touts and green beans with broccoli florets. Blanch them before stir-frying.

**5** Heat a wok until hot, add the oil and swirl it around. Add the garlic and ginger and stir-fry for 1 minute. Add the beans and stir-fry for 2–3 minutes, then add the mange-touts, spring onions and pak choi. Stir-fry for 2–3 minutes.

**6** Add the sauce to the wok and cook, stirring, until it has thickened and the vegetables are tender but crisp. Taste and adjust the seasoning, if necessary. Serve at once with the fish balls.

# Red Snapper with Ginger and Spring Onions

This is a classic Chinese way of cooking fish. Pouring the oil slowly over the spring onions and ginger allows it to partially cook them, enhancing their flavour.

*Serves 2-3*

INGREDIENTS
1 red snapper, about
  675-900 g/1½-2 lb, cleaned and
  scaled with head left on
1 bunch spring onions, cut into
  thin shreds
2.5 cm/1 in piece fresh root
  ginger, cut into thin shreds
1.5 ml/¼ tsp salt
1.5 ml/¼ tsp caster sugar
45 ml/3 tbsp groundnut oil
5 ml/1 tsp sesame oil
30-45 ml/2-3 tbsp light soy sauce
spring onion brushes, to garnish

*spring onions*

*ginger*

*groundnut oil*

*sesame oil*

*red snapper*

*light soy sauce*

*caster sugar*

## COOK'S TIP
If the fish is too big to fit inside the steamer, cut off the head and place it alongside the body – it can then be reassembled after it is cooked for serving.

**1** Rinse the fish, then pat dry with kitchen paper. Slash the flesh diagonally, three times on each side. Set the fish on a heatproof oval plate that will fit inside your bamboo steamer.

**2** Tuck about one-third of the spring onions and ginger inside the body cavity. Place the plate inside the steamer, cover with its lid, then place in a wok.

**3** Steam over a medium heat for 10–15 minutes until the fish flakes easily when tested with the tip of a knife.

**4** Carefully remove the plate from the steamer. Sprinkle over the salt, sugar and remaining spring onions and ginger.

**5** Heat the oils in a small pan until very hot, then slowly pour over the fish.

**6** Drizzle over the soy sauce and serve at once, garnished with spring onion brushes.

# Sweet-and-sour Fish

The combination of sweet and sour is a popular one in many cuisines. The sauce can be made up to two days in advance.

*Serves 3-4*

INGREDIENTS
450 g/1 lb white fish fillets, skinned, boned and cubed
2.5 ml/½ tsp Chinese five-spice powder
5 ml/1 tsp light soy sauce
1 egg, lightly beaten
30–45 ml/2–3 tbsp cornflour
groundnut oil, for deep-frying

FOR THE SAUCE
10 ml/2 tsp cornflour
60 ml/4 tbsp water
60 ml/4 tbsp pineapple juice
45 ml/3 tbsp Chinese rice vinegar
45 ml/3 tbsp caster sugar
10 ml/2 tsp light soy sauce
30 ml/2 tbsp tomato ketchup
10 ml/2 tsp Chinese rice wine or medium-dry sherry
45 ml/3 tbsp groundnut oil
1 garlic clove, crushed
15 ml/1 tbsp chopped fresh root ginger
6 spring onions, sliced diagonally into 5 cm/2 in lengths
1 green pepper, seeded and cut into 2 cm/¾ in pieces
115 g/4 oz fresh pineapple, cut into 2cm/¾ in pieces
salt and ground black pepper

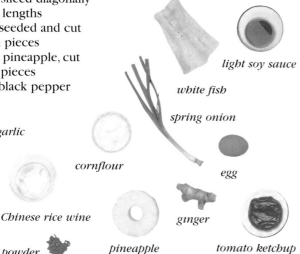

*light soy sauce*

*white fish*

*spring onion*

*garlic*

*cornflour*

*egg*

*green pepper*

*Chinese rice wine*

*ginger*

*Chinese five-spice powder*

*pineapple*

*tomato ketchup*

**1** Put the fish in a bowl. Sprinkle over the five-spice powder and soy sauce, then toss gently. Cover and leave to marinate for about 30 minutes. Dip the fish in the egg, then in the cornflour, shaking off any excess.

**2** Half-fill a wok with oil and heat to 190°C/375°F. Deep fry the fish in batches for about 2 minutes until golden. Drain and keep warm. Carefully pour off all the oil from the wok and wipe clean.

**4** Heat the wok until hot, add 30 ml/ 2 tbsp of the oil and swirl it around. Add the garlic and ginger and stir-fry for a few seconds. Add the spring onions and green pepper and stir-fry over a medium heat for 2 minutes. Add the pineapple.

COOK'S TIP
When buying the fish for this dish, select fillets which are 2 cm/¾ in or more thick.

**3** To make the sauce, blend together in a bowl the cornflour, water, pineapple juice, rice vinegar, sugar, soy sauce, ketchup and rice wine or sherry. Mix well, then set aside.

**5** Pour in the sauce and cook, stirring until thickened. Stir in the remaining 15 ml/1 tbsp oil and add seasoning to taste. Pour the sauce over the fish and serve at once.

# Green Seafood Curry

This curry is based on a Thai classic. The lovely green colour is imparted by the finely chopped chilli and fresh herbs added during the last few moments of cooking.

## Serves 4

INGREDIENTS
225 g/8 oz small ready-
  prepared squid
225 g/8 oz raw tiger prawns
400 ml/14 fl oz/1¾ cups
  coconut milk
30 ml/2 tbsp green curry paste
2 fresh kaffir lime leaves,
  finely shredded
30 ml/2 tbsp Thai fish sauce
  (*nam pla*)
450 g/1 lb firm white fish fillets,
  skinned, boned and cut into
  chunks
2 fresh green chillies, seeded and
  finely chopped
30 ml/2 tbsp torn basil or
  coriander leaves
squeeze of lime juice
Thai jasmine rice, to serve

*prawns*

*green chillies*

*squid*

*white fish*

*basil*

*coconut milk*

*green curry paste*

*kaffir lime leaves*

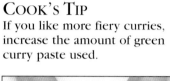

COOK'S TIP
If you like more fiery curries, increase the amount of green curry paste used.

**1** Rinse the squid and pat dry with kitchen paper. Cut the bodies into rings and halve the tentacles, if necessary.

**2** Heat a wok until hot, add the prawns and stir-fry without any oil for about 4 minutes until they turn pink.

**3** Remove the prawns from the heat and when they are cool enough to handle, peel off the shells. Make a slit along the back of each one and remove the dark black vein.

**4** Pour the coconut milk into the wok, then bring to the boil, stirring. Add the curry paste, shredded lime leaves and fish sauce. Reduce the heat to a simmer and cook for about 10 minutes, enough for the flavours to develop.

**5** Add the squid, prawns and white fish and cook for about 2 minutes until the seafood is tender. Take care not to overcook the squid as it will become tough very quickly.

**6** Just before serving, stir in the chillies and basil or coriander. Taste and adjust the flavour with a squeeze of lime juice. Serve with Thai jasmine rice.

# Squid with Peppers in a Black Bean Sauce

Salted black beans add a traditionally Chinese flavour to this tasty stir-fry.

*Serves 4*

INGREDIENTS

30 ml/2 tbsp salted black beans
30 ml/2 tbsp medium-dry sherry
15 ml/1 tbsp light soy sauce
5 ml/1 tsp cornflour
2.5 ml/½ tsp sugar
30 ml/2 tbsp water
45 ml/3 tbsp groundnut oil
450 g/1 lb ready-prepared squid,
    scored and cut into thick strips
5 ml/1 tsp finely chopped fresh
    root ginger
1 garlic clove, finely chopped
1 fresh green chilli, seeded
    and sliced
6–8 spring onions, cut diagonally
    into 2.5 cm/1 in lengths
½ red and ½ green pepper,
    cored seeded and cut into
    2.5 cm/1 in diamonds
75g/3 oz shiitake mushrooms,
    thickly sliced

*spring onions*

*shiitake mushrooms*

*medium-dry sherry*

*light soy sauce*

*ginger*

*red pepper*

*squid*

*salted black beans*  *green pepper*  *green chilli*

**1** Rinse and finely chop the black beans. Place them in a bowl with the sherry, soy sauce, cornflour, sugar and water; mix well.

**2** Heat a wok until hot, add the oil and swirl it around. When the oil is very hot, add the squid and stir-fry for 1–1½ minutes until opaque and curled at the edges. Remove with a slotted spoon and set aside.

**3** Add the ginger, garlic and chilli to the wok and stir-fry for a few seconds. Add the spring onions, peppers and mushrooms, then stir-fry for 2 minutes.

**4** Return the squid to the wok with the sauce. Cook, stirring, for about 1 minute until thickened. Serve at once.

# Spiced Scallops in their Shells

Scallops are excellent steamed. When served with this spicy sauce, they make a delicious yet simple starter. Each person spoons sauce on to the scallops before eating them.

*Serves 4*

INGREDIENTS

8 scallops, shelled (ask the fishmonger to reserve the cupped side of 4 shells)
2 slices fresh root ginger, shredded
½ garlic clove, shredded
2 spring onions, green parts only, shredded
salt and pepper

FOR THE SAUCE
1 garlic clove, crushed
15 ml/1 tbsp grated fresh root ginger
2 spring onions, white parts only, chopped
1–2 fresh green chillies, seeded and finely chopped
15 ml/1 tbsp light soy sauce
15 ml/1 tbsp dark soy sauce
10 ml/2 tsp sesame oil

*scallops*

*ginger*

*spring onions*

*garlic*

*light soy sauce*

*dark soy sauce*

*green chilli*

*sesame oil*

**1** Remove the dark beard-like fringe and tough muscle from the scallops.

**2** Place 2 scallops in each shell. Season lightly with salt and pepper, then scatter the ginger, garlic and spring onions on top. Place the shells in a bamboo steamer and steam for about 6 minutes until the scallops look opaque (you may have to do this in batches).

**3** Meanwhile, mix together all the sauce ingredients and pour into a small serving bowl.

**4** Carefully remove each shell from the steamer, taking care not to spill the juices, and arrange them on a serving plate with the sauce bowl in the centre. Serve at once.

# Lemon-grass-and-basil-scented Mussels

Thai flavourings of lemon grass and basil are used in this quick and easy dish.

*Serves 4*

INGREDIENTS
1.75 kg/4–4½ lb fresh mussels
  in the shell
2 lemon grass stalks
handful of small fresh basil leaves
5 cm/2 in piece fresh root ginger
2 shallots, finely chopped
150 ml/¼ pint/⅔ cup fish stock

*lemon grass*

*mussels*

*fish stock*

*shallots*

*ginger*

*basil*

**1** Scrub the mussels under cold running water, scraping off any barnacles with a small sharp knife. Pull or cut off the hairy "beards". Discard any with damaged shells and any that remain open when sharply tapped.

**2** Cut each lemon grass stalk in half and bruise with a rolling pin.

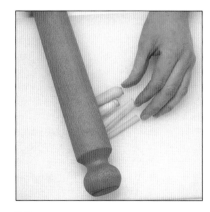

**3** Roughly chop half the basil leaves; reserve the remainder for the garnish.

**4** Put the mussels, lemon grass, chopped basil, ginger, shallots and stock in a wok. Bring to the boil, cover and simmer for 5 minutes. Discard any mussels that remain closed. Scatter over the reserved basil and serve at once.

## COOK'S TIP
Mussels are best bought fresh and eaten on the day of purchase. Any that remain closed after cooking should be thrown away.

# Spiced Prawns with Coconut

This spicy dish is based on *Sambal Goreng Udang*, which is Indonesian in origin. It is best served with plain boiled rice.

*Serves 3-4*

INGREDIENTS
2-3 fresh red chillies, seeded
    and chopped
3 shallots, chopped
1 lemon grass stalk, chopped
2 garlic cloves, chopped
thin sliver of dried shrimp paste
2.5 ml/½ tsp ground galangal
5 ml/1 tsp ground turmeric
5 ml/1 tsp ground coriander
15 ml/1 tbsp groundnut oil
250 ml/8 fl oz/1 cup water
2 fresh kaffir lime leaves
5 ml/1 tsp light brown soft sugar
2 tomatoes, peeled, seeded
    and chopped
250 ml/8 fl oz/1 cup coconut milk
675 g/1½ lb large raw prawns,
    peeled and deveined
squeeze of lemon juice
salt, to taste
shredded spring onions and
    flaked coconut, to garnish

 In a mortar pound the chillies, shallots, lemon grass, garlic, shrimp paste, galangal, turmeric and coriander with a pestle until it forms a paste.

*lemon grass*

*garlic*

*dried shrimp paste*

*turmeric*

*red chillies*

*prawns*

*coriander*

*galangal*

*groundnut oil*

*coconut milk*   *sugar*

*tomatoes*

*shallots*

*kaffir lime leaves*

### COOK'S TIP
Dried shrimp paste, much used in South-east Asia, is available from oriental stores.

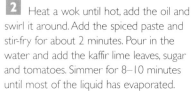 Heat a wok until hot, add the oil and swirl it around. Add the spiced paste and stir-fry for about 2 minutes. Pour in the water and add the kaffir lime leaves, sugar and tomatoes. Simmer for 8–10 minutes until most of the liquid has evaporated.

**3** Add the coconut milk and prawns and cook gently, stirring, for about 4 minutes until the prawns are pink. Taste and adjust the seasoning with salt and a squeeze of lemon juice. Serve at once, garnished with shredded spring onions and toasted flaked coconut.

# Beef Rendang

In this curry from Indonesia, the meat is simmered in a mixture of coconut milk and spices until the liquid has almost disappeared, leaving dark, intensely flavoured meat.

COOK'S TIP
This curry tastes even better if made the day before and kept covered in the fridge. Reheat it on top of the stove until piping hot before serving.

*Serves 4*

INGREDIENTS
4 dried red chillies
7.5 cm/3 in piece galangal
6 shallots, chopped
1 small red pepper, seeded and chopped
4 garlic cloves, chopped
10 ml/2 tsp ground cinnamon
10 ml/2 tsp ground coriander
5 ml/1 tsp ground turmeric
5 ml/1 tsp ground cloves
15 ml/1 tbsp groundnut oil
1.5 litres/2½ pints/6¼ cups coconut milk
2 bay leaves
2 lemon grass stalks, bruised
3 fresh kaffir lime leaves
1 kg/2¼ lb stewing or braising steak, trimmed and cut into 5 cm/2 in cubes
5 ml/1 tsp salt
shredded kaffir lime leaves and red chilli flowers, to garnish
plain boiled rice, to serve

*coriander* *cloves* *cinnamon* *turmeric* *steak* *coconut milk* *shallots* *red pepper* *garlic* *red chillies* *galangal* *bay leaves* *kaffir lime leaves* *lemon grass*

**1** Crumble or break the chillies into a bowl. Add 60 ml/4 tbsp water and leave to soak for 30 minutes.

**2** Peel and roughly chop the galangal.

**3** Put the soaked chillies and their liquid, the galangal, the chopped shallots, pepper, garlic and remaining spices into a blender or food processor and blend until smooth.

**4** Heat a wok until hot, add the oil and swirl it around. Add the spice paste and stir-fry for about 2 minutes. Pour in the coconut milk and add the bay leaves, lemon grass and kaffir lime leaves. Bring to the boil, stirring constantly.

**5** Add the meat and salt. Reduce the heat and simmer, uncovered for 2–2½ hours, stirring occasionally, until most of the liquid has evaporated. Towards the end of cooking, stir the meat more frequently to prevent it sticking. Taste and season if necessary. Garnish with shredded kaffir lime leaves and red chilli flowers. Serve with plain boiled rice.

# Paper-thin Lamb with Spring Onions

Spring onions lend a delicious flavour to the lamb in this simple supper dish.

*Serves 3-4*

INGREDIENTS

450 g/1 lb lamb fillet
30 ml/2 tbsp Chinese rice wine
10 ml/2 tsp light soy sauce
2.5 ml/½ tsp roasted and ground
 Szechuan peppercorns
2.5 ml/½ tsp salt
2.5 m/½ tsp dark brown soft sugar
20 ml/4 tsp dark soy sauce
15 ml/1 tbsp sesame oil
30 ml/2 tbsp groundnut oil
2 garlic cloves, thinly sliced
2 bunches spring onions, cut
 into 7.5 cm/3 in lengths,
 then shredded
30 ml/2 tbsp chopped
 fresh coriander

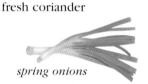
*spring onions*

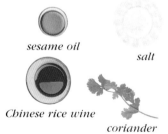
*lamb*          *dark soy sauce*

*sesame oil*          *salt*

*Chinese rice wine*          *coriander*

*groundnut oil*          *garlic*

**1** Wrap the lamb and place in the freezer for about 1 hour until just frozen. Cut the meat across the grain into paper-thin slices. Put the lamb slices in a bowl, add 10 ml/2 tsp of the rice wine, the light soy sauce and ground Szechuan peppercorns. Mix well and leave to marinate for 15–30 minutes.

**2** Make the sauce: in a bowl mix together the remaining rice wine, the salt, brown sugar, dark soy sauce and 10ml/2 tsp of the sesame oil. Set aside.

**3** Heat a wok until hot, add the oil and swirl it around. Add the garlic and let it sizzle for a few seconds, then add the lamb. Stir-fry for about 1 minute until the lamb is no longer pink. Pour in the sauce and stir briefly.

**4** Add the spring onions and coriander and stir-fry for 15–20 seconds until the spring onions just wilt. The finished dish should be slightly dry in appearance. Serve at once, sprinkled with the remaining sesame oil.

# Chilli Beef with Basil

This is a dish for chilli lovers! It is very easy to prepare and cook.

*Serves 2*

INGREDIENTS
about 90 ml/6 tbsp groundnut oil
16–20 large fresh basil leaves
275 g/10 oz rump steak
30 ml/2 tbsp Thai fish sauce
    (*nam pla*)
5 ml/1 tsp dark brown soft sugar
1–2 fresh red chillies, sliced
    into rings
3 garlic cloves, chopped
5 ml/1 tsp chopped fresh
    root ginger
1 shallot, thinly sliced
30 ml/2 tbsp finely chopped fresh
    basil leaves
squeeze of lemon juice
salt and ground black pepper
Thai jasmine rice, to serve

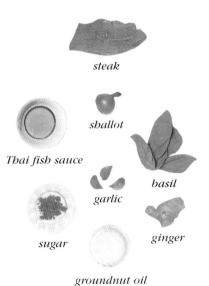

*steak*

*shallot*

*Thai fish sauce*

*basil*

*garlic*

*sugar*

*ginger*

*groundnut oil*

*red chilli*

**1** Heat the oil in a wok and, when hot, add the basil leaves and fry for about 1 minute until crisp and golden. Drain on kitchen paper. Remove the wok from the heat and pour off all but 30 ml/2 tbsp of the oil.

**2** Cut the steak across the grain into thin strips. In a bowl mix together the fish sauce and sugar. Add the beef, mix well, then leave to marinate for about 30 minutes.

**3** Reheat the oil until hot, add the chilli(es), garlic, ginger and shallot and stir-fry for 30 seconds. Add the beef and chopped basil, then stir-fry for about 3 minutes. Flavour with lemon juice and add seasoning to taste.

**4** Transfer to a serving plate, scatter over the basil leaves and serve immediately with Thai jasmine rice.

# Lemon Grass Pork

Chillies and lemon grass flavour this simple stir-fry, while peanuts add crunch.

*Serves 4*

INGREDIENTS

675 g/1½ lb boneless loin of pork
2 lemon grass stalks,
   finely chopped
4 spring onions, thinly sliced
5 ml/1 tsp salt
12 black peppercorns,
   coarsely crushed
30 ml/2 tbsp groundnut oil
2 garlic cloves, chopped
2 fresh red chillies, seeded
   and chopped
5 ml/1 tsp light brown soft sugar
30 ml/2 tbsp Thai fish sauce
   (*nam pla*), or to taste
25 g/1 oz/¼ cup roasted
   unsalted peanuts, chopped
salt and ground black pepper
rice noodles, to serve
roughly torn coriander leaves,
   to garnish

*spring onions*

*red chillies*

*peanuts*

*pork*

*sugar*

*lemon grass*

*coriander*

*Thai fish sauce*

*garlic*

*groundnut oil*

**1** Trim any excess fat from the pork. Cut the meat across into 5 mm/¼ in thick slices, then cut each slice into 5 mm/¼ in strips. Put the pork into a bowl with the lemon grass, spring onions, salt and crushed peppercorns; mix well. Cover and leave to marinate for 30 minutes.

**2** Heat a wok until hot, add the oil and swirl it around. Add the pork mixture and stir-fry for 3 minutes.

**3** Add the garlic and chillies and stir-fry for a further 5–8 minutes over a medium heat until the pork no longer looks pink.

**4** Add the sugar, fish sauce and peanuts, and toss to mix. Taste and adjust the seasoning, if necessary. Serve at once on a bed of rice noodles, garnished with roughly torn coriander leaves.

# Spiced Lamb with Spinach

This recipe is based on *Sag Gosht* – meat cooked with spinach. The whole spices in this dish are not meant to be eaten.

### Serves 3-4

INGREDIENTS

45 ml/3 tbsp vegetable oil
500 g/1¼ lb lean boneless lamb,
    cut into 2.5 cm/1 in cubes
1 onion, chopped
3 garlic cloves, finely chopped
1 cm/½ in piece fresh root
    ginger, finely chopped
6 black peppercorns
4 whole cloves
1 bay leaf
3 green cardamom pods, crushed
5 ml/1 tsp ground cumin
5 ml/1 tsp ground coriander
generous pinch of
    cayenne pepper
150 ml/¼ pint/⅔ cup water
2 tomatoes, peeled, seeded
    and chopped
5 ml/1 tsp salt
400 g/14 oz fresh spinach,
    trimmed, washed and
    finely chopped
5 ml/1 tsp garam masala
crisp-fried onions and fresh
    coriander sprigs, to garnish
naan bread or spiced basmati
    rice, to serve

*cloves*
*lamb*
*garlic*
*onion*
*cardamom pods*
*coriander*
*cayenne pepper*
*cumin*
*garam masala*
*bay leaf*
*spinach*
*ginger*
*tomatoes*

**1** Heat a karahi or wok until hot. Add 30 ml/2 tbsp of the oil and swirl it around. When hot, stir-fry the lamb in batches until evenly browned. Remove the lamb and set aside. Add the remaining oil, onion, garlic and ginger and stir-fry for 2–3 minutes.

**2** Add the peppercorns, cloves, bay leaf, cardamom pods, cumin, coriander and cayenne pepper. Stir-fry for 30–45 seconds. Return the lamb and add the water, tomatoes and salt and bring to the boil. Simmer, covered, over a very low heat for about 1 hour, stirring occasionally until the meat is tender.

**3** Increase the heat, then gradually add the spinach to the lamb, stirring to mix. Keep stirring and cooking until the spinach wilts completely and most, but not all of the liquid has evaporated and you are left with a thick green sauce. Stir in the garam masala. Garnish with crisp-fried onions and coriander sprigs. Serve with naan bread or spiced basmati rice.

# Glazed Chicken with Cashew Nuts

Hoisin sauce lends a sweet yet slightly hot note to this chicken dish, while cashew nuts add a pleasing contrast of texture.

**VARIATION**
Use blanched almonds instead of cashew nuts if you prefer.

## Serves 4

INGREDIENTS
75 g/3 oz/¾ cup cashew nuts
1 red pepper
450 g/1 lb skinless and boneless
   chicken breasts
45 ml/3 tbsp groundnut oil
4 garlic cloves, finely chopped
30 ml/2 tbsp Chinese rice wine
   or medium-dry sherry
45 ml/3 tbsp hoisin sauce
10 ml/2 tsp sesame oil
5-6 spring onions, green parts
   only, cut into
     2.5 cm/1 in lengths

*chicken*

*spring onion*

*red pepper*

*cashew nuts*

*Chinese rice wine*

*garlic*

*groundnut oil*

*hoisin sauce*

*sesame oil*

**1** Heat a wok until hot, add the cashew nuts and stir-fry over a low to medium heat for 1–2 minutes until golden brown. Remove and set aside.

**2** Halve the pepper and remove the seeds. Slice the pepper and chicken into finger-length strips.

**3** Heat the wok again until hot, add the oil and swirl it around. Add the garlic and let it sizzle in the oil for a few seconds. Add the pepper and chicken and stir-fry for 2 minutes.

**4** Add the rice wine or sherry and hoisin sauce. Continue to stir-fry until the chicken is tender and all the ingredients are evenly glazed.

**5** Stir in the sesame oil, toasted cashew nuts and spring onion tips. Serve immediately with rice or noodles.

# Thai Red Chicken Curry

Here chicken and potatoes are simmered in spiced coconut milk, then garnished with shredded kaffir lime leaves and red chillies.

## Serves 4

INGREDIENTS
1 onion
15 ml/1 tbsp groundnut oil
400 ml/14 fl oz/1⅔ cups
    coconut milk
30 ml/2 tbsp red curry paste
30 ml/2 tbsp Thai fish sauce
    (*nam pla*)
15 ml/1 tbsp soft light
    brown sugar
225 g/8 oz tiny new potatoes
450 g/1 lb skinless chicken
    breasts, cut into chunks
15 ml/1 tbsp lime juice
30 ml/2 tbsp chopped fresh mint
15 ml/1 tbsp chopped fresh basil
2 kaffir lime leaves, shredded
1-2 fresh red chillies, seeded and
    finely shredded
salt and ground black pepper

*lime*

*sugar*

*new potatoes*

*basil*        *chicken*

*red curry paste*

*onion*

*coconut milk*

*mint*

*Thai fish sauce*

**VARIATION**
You can use boneless chicken thighs instead of breasts. Simply skin them, cut the flesh into chunks and cook in the coconut milk with the potatoes.

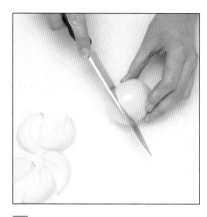

**1** Cut the onion into wedges.

**2** Heat a wok until hot, add the oil and swirl it around. Add the onion and stir-fry for 3–4 minutes.

**3** Pour in the coconut milk, then bring to the boil, stirring. Stir in the curry paste, fish sauce and sugar.

**4** Add the potatoes and seasoning and simmer gently, covered, for about 20 minutes.

**5** Add the chicken chunks and cook, covered, over a low heat for a further 5–10 minutes until the chicken and potatoes are tender.

**6** Stir in the lime juice, chopped mint and basil. Serve at once, sprinkled with the shredded kaffir lime leaves and red chillies.

# Balti Chicken Tikka Masala

This recipe is based on *Makkhani Murghi*, a popular Balti dish. Serve with warm naan bread or fluffy basmati rice.

*Serves 4*

INGREDIENTS
FOR THE MARINATED CHICKEN
4 part-boned chicken breasts, skinned
150 ml/¼ pint/⅔ cup natural yogurt
2.5 cm/1 in piece fresh root ginger, grated
2 garlic cloves, crushed
5 ml/1 tsp chilli powder
15 ml/1 tbsp ground coriander
30 ml/2 tbsp vegetable oil
30 ml/2 tbsp lime juice
few drops each of yellow and red liquid food colouring, mixed to a bright orange shade

FOR THE MASALA
75 g/3 oz unsalted butter
15 ml/1 tbsp vegetable oil
1 onion, chopped
450 g/1 lb tomatoes, peeled, seeded and chopped
5 ml/1 tsp salt
1 fresh green chilli, seeded and finely chopped
5 ml/1 tsp garam masala
1.5 ml/¼ tsp cayenne pepper
120 ml/4 fl oz/½ cup double cream
45 ml/3 tbsp natural yogurt
30 ml/2 tbsp roughly torn fresh coriander leaves
5 ml/1 tsp dry-roasted cumin seeds

**COOK'S TIP**
If you can, leave the chicken to marinate for as long as possible to allow plenty of time for it to absorb the flavourings.

chilli powder
chicken
coriander
tomatoes
double cream
butter
cayenne pepper
ginger
green chilli
food colouring
yogurt
vegetable oil
onion
coriander

**1** Cut each chicken breast into three or four pieces, then slash the meaty side of each piece. Put the chicken into a shallow dish. In a bowl, mix together the yogurt, ginger, garlic, chilli powder, ground coriander, oil, lime juice and colouring. Pour over the chicken and toss to coat completely, making sure that the marinade goes into the slits in the chicken. Cover and leave in the fridge for 6–24 hours, turning occasionally.

**2** Preheat the oven to 230°C/450°F/Gas 8. Lift the chicken pieces out of the marinade, shaking off any excess, and arrange in a shallow baking tin. Bake for 15–20 minutes until golden brown and cooked through.

**3** Meanwhile, make the masala: heat the butter and oil in a karahi or wok, add the onion and fry for 5 minutes until softened. Add the tomatoes, salt, chilli, garam masala and cayenne pepper. Cook, covered, for about 10 minutes.

**4** Stir in the cream and yogurt, then simmer over a low heat for 1–2 minutes, stirring constantly. Add the chicken pieces, then stir to coat in the sauce. Serve at once sprinkled with coriander leaves and roasted cumin seeds.

# Stir-fried Turkey with Broccoli and Mushrooms

This is a really easy, tasty supper dish which works well with chicken too.

*Serves 4*

INGREDIENTS

115 g/4 oz broccoli florets
4 spring onions
5 ml/1 tsp cornflour
45 ml/3 tbsp oyster sauce
15 ml/1 tbsp dark soy sauce
120 ml/4 fl oz/½ cup
  chicken stock
10 ml/2 tsp lemon juice
45 ml/3 tbsp groundnut oil
450 g/1 lb turkey steaks, cut into
  strips, about 5 mm x 5 cm/
  ¼ x 2 in
1 small onion, chopped
2 garlic cloves, crushed
10 ml/2 tsp grated fresh
  root ginger
115 g/4 oz fresh shiitake
  mushrooms, sliced
75 g/3 oz baby sweetcorn,
  halved lengthways
15 ml/1 tbsp sesame oil
salt and ground black pepper
egg noodles, to serve

*onion*

*broccoli*

*spring onion*

*oyster sauce*   *turkey*   *mushrooms*

*lemon*

*dark soy sauce*

*groundnut oil*

*garlic*

*baby sweetcorn*

*chicken stock*

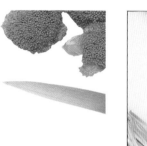

**1** Divide the broccoli florets into smaller sprigs and cut the stalks into thin diagonal slices.

**2** Finely chop the white parts of the spring onions and slice the green parts into thin shreds.

**3** In a bowl, blend together the cornflour, oyster sauce, soy sauce, stock and lemon juice. Set aside.

**4** Heat a wok until hot, add 30 ml/ 2 tbsp of the groundnut oil and swirl it around. Add the turkey and stir-fry for about 2 minutes until golden and crispy at the edges. Remove the turkey from the wok and keep warm.

**5** Add the remaining groundnut oil to the wok and stir-fry the chopped onion, garlic and ginger over a medium heat for about 1 minute. Increase the heat to high, add the broccoli, mushrooms and sweetcorn and stir-fry for 2 minutes.

**6** Return the turkey to the wok, then add the sauce with the chopped spring onion and seasoning. Cook, stirring, for about 1 minute until the sauce has thickened. Stir in the sesame oil. Serve immediately on a bed of egg noodles with the finely shredded spring onion scattered on top.

# Sweet-sour Duck with Mango

Mango adds natural sweetness to this colourful stir-fry. Crispy deep-fried noodles make the perfect accompaniment.

## VARIATION
If baby aubergines are not available, use one small to medium aubergine instead.

## Serves 4

INGREDIENTS
225–350 g/8–12 oz duck breasts
45 ml/3 tbsp dark soy sauce
15 ml/1 tbsp Chinese rice wine
5 ml/1 tsp sesame oil
5 ml/1 tsp Chinese five-
  spice powder
15 ml/1 tbsp soft brown sugar
10 ml/2 tsp cornflour
45 ml/3 tbsp Chinese rice vinegar
15 ml/1 tbsp tomato ketchup
1 mango, not too ripe
3 baby aubergines
1 red onion
1 carrot
60 ml/4 tbsp groundnut oil
1 garlic clove, sliced
2.5 cm/1 in piece fresh root
  ginger, cut into shreds
75 g/3 oz sugar snap peas

**1** Thinly slice the duck breasts and place in a bowl. Mix together 15 ml/ 1 tbsp of the soy sauce with the rice wine or sherry, sesame oil and five-spice powder. Pour over the duck, cover and leave to marinate for 1–2 hours. In a separate bowl, blend together the sugar, cornflour, rice vinegar, ketchup and remaining soy sauce. Set aside.

**2** Peel the mango, slice the flesh from the stone, then cut into thick strips. Slice the aubergines, onion and carrot into similar-sized pieces.

**3** Heat a wok until hot, add 30 ml/ 2 tbsp of the oil and swirl it around. Drain the duck, reserving the marinade. Stir-fry the duck slices over a high heat until the fat is crisp and golden. Remove and keep warm. Add 15 ml/1 tbsp of the oil to the wok and stir-fry the aubergine for 3 minutes until golden.

groundnut oil

duck breasts

carrot

dark soy sauce

Chinese rice wine

aubergines

mango

sesame oil

sugar snap peas

ginger

sugar

red onion

garlic

tomato ketchup

Chinese five-spice powder

**4** Add the remaining oil and fry the onion, garlic, ginger and carrot for 2–3 minutes, then add the sugar snap peas and stir-fry for a further 2 minutes.

**5** Add the mango and return the duck with the sauce and reserved marinade to the wok. Cook, stirring, until the sauce thickens slightly. Serve at once.

# VEGETABLE AND VEGETARIAN DISHES

## Stir-fried Vegetables with Coriander Omelette

This is a great supper dish for vegetarians. The glaze is added here only to make the mixture shine, it is not intended as a sauce.

*Serves 3–4*

INGREDIENTS
FOR THE OMELETTE
2 eggs
30 ml/2 tbsp water
45 ml/3 tbsp chopped
  fresh coriander
salt and ground black pepper
15 ml/1 tbsp groundnut oil

FOR THE GLAZED VEGETABLES
15 ml/1 tbsp cornflour
30 ml/2 tbsp dry sherry
15 ml/1 tbsp sweet chilli sauce
120 ml/4 fl oz/½ cup
  vegetable stock
30 ml/2 tbsp groundnut oil
5 ml/1 tsp grated fresh
  root ginger
6–8 spring onions, sliced
115 g/4 oz mange-touts
1 yellow pepper, seeded
  and sliced
115 g/4 oz fresh shiitake or
  button mushrooms
75 g/3 oz (drained weight)
  canned water chestnuts, rinsed
115 g/4 oz beansprouts
½ small Chinese cabbage,
  coarsely shredded

*egg*

*coriander*

*mange-touts*

*groundnut oil*

*spring onion*

*yellow pepper*

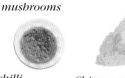

*mushrooms*

*stock*

*sweet chilli sauce*

*Chinese cabbage*

*beansprouts*

**1** Make the omelette: whisk the eggs, water, coriander and seasoning in a small bowl. Heat the oil in a wok. Pour in the eggs, then tilt the wok so that the mixture spreads to an even layer. Cook over a high heat until the edges are slightly crisp.

**2** With a wok spatula or palette knife, flip the omelette over and cook the other side for about 30 seconds until lightly browned. Turn the omelette on to a board and leave to cool. When cold, roll up loosely and cut into thin slices. Wipe the wok clean.

**3** In a bowl, blend together the cornflour, soy sauce, chilli sauce and stock. Set aside.

**4** Heat the wok until hot, add the oil and swirl it around, add the ginger and spring onions and stir-fry for a few seconds to flavour the oil. Add the mange-touts, pepper, mushrooms and water chestnuts and stir-fry for 3 minutes.

## VARIATION
Vary the combination of vegetables used according to availability and taste.

**5** Add the beansprouts and Chinese cabbage and stir-fry for 2 minutes.

**6** Pour in the glaze ingredients and cook, stirring, for about 1 minute until the glaze thickens and coats the vegetables. Turn the vegetables on to a warmed serving plate and top with the omelette shreds. Serve at once.

# Szechuan Aubergines

This dish is also known as fish-fragrant aubergine, as the aubergine is cooked with flavourings that are often used with fish.

*Serves 4*

INGREDIENTS
2 small aubergines
5 ml/1 tsp salt
3 dried red chillies
groundnut oil, for deep frying
3–4 garlic cloves, finely chopped
1 cm/½ in piece fresh root ginger,
   finely chopped
4 spring onions, cut into 2.5 cm/
   1 in lengths (white and green
   parts separated)
15 ml/1 tbsp Chinese rice wine
   or medium-dry sherry
15 ml/1 tbsp light soy sauce
5 ml/1 tsp sugar
1.5 ml/¼ tsp ground roasted
   Szechuan peppercorns
15 ml/1 tbsp Chinese rice vinegar
5 ml/1 tsp sesame oil

*ginger*

*aubergine*

*dried red chillies*

*spring onions*

*Chinese rice wine*

*light soy sauce*

*sesame oil*

*garlic*

*groundnut oil*

**1**   Trim the aubergines and cut into strips, about 4 cm/1½ in wide and 7.5 cm/3 in long. Place the aubergines in a colander and sprinkle over the salt. Leave for 30 minutes, then rinse them thoroughly under cold running water. Pat dry with kitchen paper.

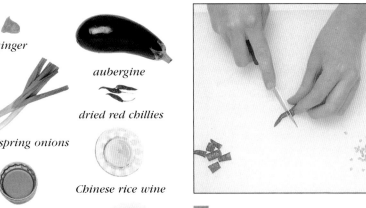

**2**   Meanwhile, soak the chillies in warm water for 15 minutes. Drain, then cut each chilli into three or four pieces, discarding the seeds.

**3**   Half-fill a wok with oil and heat to 180°C/350°F. Deep fry the aubergine until golden brown. Drain on kitchen paper. Pour off most of the oil from the wok. Reheat the oil and add the garlic, ginger and white spring onion.

**4**   Stir-fry for 30 seconds. Add the aubergine and toss, then add the rice wine or sherry, soy sauce, sugar, ground Szechuan peppercorns and rice vinegar. Stir-fry for 1–2 minutes. Sprinkle over the sesame oil and green spring onion.

# Chinese Greens with Oyster Sauce

Here Chinese greens are prepared in a very simple way – stir-fried and served with oyster sauce. The combination makes a simple, quickly prepared, tasty accompaniment.

*Serves 3-4*

INGREDIENTS
450 g/1 lb Chinese greens
  (*pak choi*)
30 ml/2 tbsp groundnut oil
15-30 ml/1-2 tbsp oyster sauce

*Chinese greens*

*groundnut oil*

*oyster sauce*

## VARIATION

You can replace the Chinese greens with Chinese flowering cabbage, which is also known by its Cantonese name *choi sam*. It has bright green leaves and tiny yellow flowers, which are also eaten along with the leaves and stalks. It is available from oriental grocers.

**1** Trim the Chinese greens, removing any discoloured leaves and damaged stems. Tear into manageable pieces.

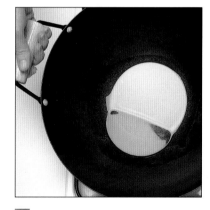

**2** Heat a wok until hot, add the oil and swirl it around.

**3** Add the Chinese greens and stir-fry for 2–3 minutes until the greens have wilted a little.

**4** Add the oyster sauce and continue to stir-fry a few seconds more until the greens are cooked but still slightly crisp. Serve immediately.

# Deep-fried Root Vegetables with Spiced Salt

All kinds of root vegetables may be finely sliced and deep-fried to make "crisps". Serve as an accompaniment to an oriental-style meal or simply by themselves as a nibble.

*Serves 4-6*

INGREDIENTS
1 carrot
2 parsnips
2 raw beetroots
1 sweet potato
groundnut oil, for deep frying
1.5 ml/¼ tsp chilli powder
5 ml/1 tsp sea salt flakes

*chilli powder*

*sweet potato*

*groundnut oil*

*carrot*

*beetroot*

*parsnips*

**1** Peel all the vegetables, then slice the carrot and parsnips into long, thin ribbons and the beetroots and sweet potato into thin rounds. Pat dry on kitchen paper.

**2** Half-fill a wok with oil and heat to 180°C/350°F. Add the vegetable slices in batches and deep-fry for 2–3 minutes until golden and crisp. Remove and drain on kitchen paper.

**3** Place the chilli powder and sea salt in a mortar and grind together to a coarse powder.

**4** Pile up the vegetable "crisps" on a serving plate and sprinkle over the spiced salt.

## COOK'S TIP
To save time you can slice the vegetables using a mandoline or a blender or food processor with a thin slicing disc attached.

# Stir-fried Spinach with Garlic and Sesame Seeds

The sesame seeds add a crunchy texture which contrasts well with the wilted spinach in this easy vegetable dish.

*Serves 2*

INGREDIENTS
225 g/8 oz fresh spinach, washed
25 ml/1½ tbsp sesame seeds
30 ml/2 tbsp groundnut oil
1.5 ml/¼ tsp sea salt flakes
2-3 garlic cloves, sliced

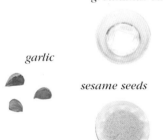

*spinach*

*groundnut oil*

*garlic*

*sesame seeds*

**1** Shake the spinach to get rid of any excess water, then remove the stalks and discard any yellow or damaged leaves. Lay several spinach leaves one on top of another, roll up tightly and cut crossways into wide strips. Repeat with the remaining leaves.

**2** Heat a wok to a medium heat, add the sesame seeds and dry fry, stirring, for 1–2 minutes until golden brown. Transfer to a small bowl and set aside.

**3** Add the oil to the wok and swirl it around. When hot, add the salt, spinach and garlic and stir-fry for 2 minutes until the spinach just wilts and the leaves are coated with the oil.

**4** Sprinkle over the sesame seeds and toss well. Serve at once.

## COOK'S TIP
Take care when adding the spinach to the hot oil as it will spit furiously.

# Yellow Flower Vegetables

To serve, each person spreads hoisin sauce on a pancake, adds filling and rolls it up.

## Serves 4

INGREDIENTS
3 eggs
30 ml/2 tbsp water
60 ml/4 tbsp groundnut oil
25 g/1 oz dried Chinese
 black mushrooms
25 g/1 oz dried wood ears
10 ml/2 tsp cornflour
30 ml/2 tbsp light soy sauce
30 ml/2 tbsp Chinese rice wine
 or medium-dry sherry
10 ml/2 tsp sesame oil
2 garlic cloves, finely chopped
1 cm/½ in piece fresh root ginger,
 cut into thin shreds
75 g/3 oz canned sliced bamboo
 shoots (drained weight), rinsed
175 g/6 oz beansprouts
4 spring onions, finely shredded
salt and ground black pepper
Chinese pancakes and hoisin
 sauce, to serve

COOK'S TIP
Chinese pancakes are available
from oriental grocers. Reheat
them in a bamboo steamer for
2–3 minutes before serving.

**1** Whisk the eggs, water and seasoning in a small bowl. Heat 15 ml/ 1 tbsp of the groundnut oil in a wok and swirl it around. Pour in the eggs, then tilt the wok so that they spread to an even layer. Continue to cook over a high heat for about 2 minutes until set. Turn on to a board and, when cool, roll up and cut into thin strips. Wipe the wok clean.

**2** Meanwhile, put the black mushrooms and wood ears into separate bowls. Pour over enough warm water to cover, then leave to soak for 20–30 minutes until soft. Drain the dried mushrooms, reserving their soaking liquid. Squeeze the excess liquid from each of them.

**3** Remove the tough stalks and thinly slice the black mushrooms. Finely shred the wood ears. Set aside. Strain the reserved soaking liquid through muslin into a jug; reserve 120 ml/4 fl oz/½ cup of the liquid. In a bowl, blend the cornflour with the reserved liquid, soy sauce, rice wine or sherry and sesame oil.

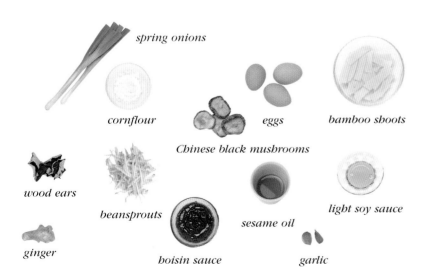

spring onions

cornflour

eggs

bamboo shoots

Chinese black mushrooms

wood ears

beansprouts

sesame oil

light soy sauce

ginger

hoisin sauce

garlic

**4** Heat the wok over a medium heat, add the remaining groundnut oil and swirl it around. Add the wood ears and black mushrooms and stir-fry for about 2 minutes. Add the garlic, ginger, bamboo shoots and beansprouts and stir-fry for 1–2 minutes.

**5** Pour in the cornflour mixture and cook, stirring, for 1 minute until thickened. Add the spring onions and omelette strips and toss gently. Adjust the seasoning, adding more soy sauce, if needed. Serve at once with the Chinese pancakes and hoisin sauce.

# Spiced Coconut Mushrooms

Here is a simple and delicious way to cook mushrooms. They may be served with almost any Asian meal as well as with grilled or roasted meats and poultry.

*Serves 3-4*

INGREDIENTS
30 ml/2 tbsp groundnut oil
2 garlic cloves, finely chopped
2 fresh red chillies, seeded and
    sliced into rings
3 shallots, finely chopped
225 g/8 oz brown-cap
    mushrooms, thickly sliced
150 ml/¼ pint/⅔ cup coconut milk
30 ml/2 tbsp chopped fresh
    coriander
salt and ground black pepper

red chillies

coconut milk

mushrooms

groundnut oil

coriander

garlic

**1** Heat a wok until hot, add the oil and swirl it around. Add the garlic and chillies, then stir-fry for a few seconds.

**2** Add the shallots and stir-fry for 2–3 minutes until softened. Add the mushrooms and stir-fry for 3 minutes.

**3** Pour in the coconut milk and bring to the boil. Boil rapidly over a high heat until the liquid is reduced by half and coats the mushrooms. Taste and adjust the seasoning, if necessary.

**4** Sprinkle over the coriander and toss gently to mix. Serve at once.

## VARIATION
Use snipped fresh chives instead of coriander if you wish.

# Spicy Potatoes and Cauliflower

This dish is simplicity itself to make and may be eaten as a vegetarian main meal for two with Indian breads or rice, a raita, such as cucumber and yogurt, and a fresh mint relish.

*Serves 2*

INGREDIENTS
225 g/8 oz potatoes
75 ml/5 tbsp groundnut oil
5 ml/1 tsp ground cumin
5 ml/1 tsp ground coriander
1.5 ml/¼ tsp ground turmeric
1.5 ml/¼ tsp cayenne pepper
1 fresh green chilli, seeded and
    finely chopped
1 medium cauliflower, broken up
    into small florets
5 ml/1 tsp cumin seeds
2 garlic cloves, cut into shreds
15–30 ml/1–2 tbsp chopped
    fresh coriander
salt, to taste

cumin seeds

potatoes

cayenne pepper

coriander

fresh
coriander

turmeric

cumin

cauliflower

garlic

green chilli

**1** Boil the potatoes in their skins in boiling salted water for about 20 minutes until just tender. Drain and leave to cool. When cool enough to handle, peel and cut into 2.5 cm/1 in cubes.

**2** Heat 45 ml/3 tbsp of the oil in a karahi or wok. When hot, add the ground cumin, coriander, turmeric, cayenne pepper and chilli. Let the spices sizzle for a few seconds.

**3** Add the cauliflower and about 60 ml/4 tbsp water. Cook, stirring, for 6–8 minutes over a medium heat. Add the potatoes and stir-fry for 2–3 minutes. Season to taste. Remove from the heat.

**4** Heat the remaining oil in a small frying pan. When hot, add the cumin seeds and garlic and cook until lightly browned. Pour the mixture over the vegetables. Sprinkle with the chopped fresh coriander and serve at once.

# Red-cooked Tofu with Chinese Mushrooms

Red-cooked is a term applied to Chinese dishes cooked with dark soy sauce. This tasty dish can be served as either a side dish or main meal.

*Serves 2-4*

INGREDIENTS
225 g/8 oz firm tofu
45 ml/3 tbsp dark soy sauce
30 ml/2 tbsp Chinese rice wine
  or medium-dry sherry
10 ml/2 tsp soft dark brown sugar
1 garlic clove, crushed
15 ml/1 tbsp grated fresh
  root ginger
2.5 ml/½ tsp Chinese five-
  spice powder
pinch of ground roasted
  Szechuan peppercorns
6 dried Chinese black mushrooms
5 ml/1 tsp cornflour
30 ml/2 tbsp groundnut oil
5-6 spring onions, sliced into
  2.5 cm/1 in lengths
rice noodles, to serve
small basil leaves, to garnish

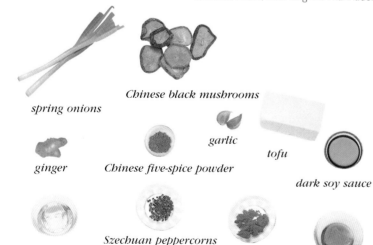

*Chinese black mushrooms*

*spring onions*

*ginger*

*garlic*

*tofu*

*Chinese five-spice powder*

*dark soy sauce*

*Chinese rice wine*

*Szechuan peppercorns*

*sugar*

*groundnut oil*

**1** Drain the tofu, pat dry with kitchen paper and cut into 2.5cm/1 in cubes. Place in a shallow dish. In a small bowl, mix together the soy sauce, rice wine or sherry, sugar, garlic, ginger, five-spice powder and Szechuan peppercorns. Pour the marinade over the tofu, toss well and leave to marinate for about 30 minutes. Drain, reserving the marinade.

**2** Meanwhile, soak the dried black mushrooms in warm water for 20–30 minutes until soft. Drain, reserving 90 ml/6 tbsp of the soaking liquid. Squeeze out any excess liquid from the mushrooms, remove the tough stalks and slice the caps. In a small bowl, blend the cornflour with the reserved marinade and mushroom soaking liquid.

**3** Heat a wok until hot, add the oil and swirl it around. Add the tofu and fry for 2–3 minutes until evenly golden. Remove from the wok and set aside.

**4** Add the mushrooms and white spring onions to the wok and stir-fry for 2 minutes. Pour in the marinade mixture and stir for 1 minute until thickened.

**5** Return the tofu to the wok with the green spring onions. Simmer gently for 1–2 minutes. Serve at once with rice noodles and scattered with basil leaves.

# Spicy Chick-Peas with Fresh Ginger

Chick-peas are filling, nourishing and cheap. Here they are served with a refreshing raita made with spring onions and mint. Serve as a snack or as part of a main meal.

*Serves 4-6*

### INGREDIENTS

225 g/8 oz dried chick-peas
30 ml/2 tbsp vegetable oil
1 small onion, chopped
4 cm/1½ in piece fresh root
    ginger, finely chopped
2 garlic cloves, finely chopped
1.5 ml/¼ tsp ground turmeric
450 g/1 lb tomatoes, peeled,
    seeded and chopped
30 ml/2 tbsp chopped
    fresh coriander
10 ml/2 tsp garam masala
salt and pepper
fresh coriander sprigs, to garnish

### FOR THE RAITA

150 ml/¼ pint/⅔ cup yogurt
2 spring onions, finely chopped
5 ml/1 tsp roasted cumin seeds
30 ml/2 tbsp chopped fresh mint
pinch of cayenne pepper,
    or to taste

### VARIATION

You can replace the dried chick-peas with 2 x 425g/15oz cans chick-peas. Drain and rinse thoroughly before adding to the tomatoes in step 3.

**1** Put the chick-peas in a large bowl and pour over enough cold water to cover. Leave to soak overnight. The next day, drain the chick-peas and put them in a large pan with fresh cold water to cover. Bring to the boil, then boil hard for 10 minutes. Lower the heat and simmer gently for 1½–2 hours until tender. Drain well.

**2** Heat a karahi or wok until hot, add the oil and swirl it around. Add the onion and stir-fry for 2–3 minutes, then add the ginger, garlic and turmeric. Stir-fry for a few seconds more.

**3** Add the tomatoes, chick-peas and seasoning, bring to the boil, then simmer for 10–15 until the tomatoes have reduced to a thick sauce.

coriander   onion

tomatoes

turmeric

spring onions

garlic

mint

natural yogurt

chick-peas

ginger

garam masala

**4** Meanwhile, make the raita: mix together the yogurt, spring onions, roasted cumin seeds, mint and cayenne pepper to taste. Set aside.

**5** Just before the end of cooking, stir the chopped coriander and garam masala into the chick-peas. Serve at once, garnished with coriander sprigs and accompanied by the raita.

# Crispy Noodles with Mixed Vegetables

In this dish, rice vermicelli noodles are deep-fried until crisp, then tossed into a colourful selection of stir-fried vegetables.

## Serves 3–4

INGREDIENTS
2 large carrots
2 courgettes
4 spring onions
115 g/4 oz yard-long beans or green beans
115 g/4 oz dried vermicelli rice noodles or cellophane noodles
groundnut oil, for deep frying
2.5 cm/1 in piece fresh root ginger, cut into shreds
1 fresh red chilli, sliced
115 g/4 oz fresh shiitake or button mushrooms, thickly sliced
few Chinese cabbage leaves, coarsely shredded
75 g/3 oz beansprouts
30 ml/2 tbsp light soy sauce
30 ml/2 tbsp Chinese rice wine
5 ml/1 tsp sugar
30 ml/2 tbsp roughly torn coriander leaves

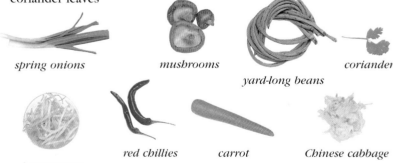

*spring onions*    *mushrooms*    *coriander*

*yard-long beans*

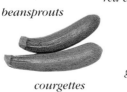
*beansprouts*

*red chillies*    *carrot*    *Chinese cabbage*

*courgettes*    *ginger*    *Chinese rice wine*    *light soy sauce*

**1** Cut the carrots and courgettes into fine sticks. Shred the spring onions into similar-size pieces. Trim the beans. If using yard-long beans, cut them into short lengths.

**2** Break the noodles into lengths of about 7.5 cm/3 in. Half-fill a wok with oil and heat it to 180°C/350°F. Deep fry the raw noodles, a handful at a time, for 1–2 minutes until puffed and crispy. Drain on kitchen paper. Carefully pour off all but 30 ml/2 tbsp of the oil.

**3** Reheat the oil in the wok. When hot, add the beans and stir-fry for 2–3 minutes. Add the ginger, red chilli, mushrooms, carrots and courgettes and stir-fry for 1–2 minutes.

**4** Add the Chinese cabbage, beansprouts and spring onions. Stir-fry for 1 minute, then add the soy sauce, rice wine and sugar. Cook, stirring, for about 30 seconds.

**5** Add the noodles and coriander and toss to mix, taking care not to crush the noodles too much. Serve at once, piled up on a plate.

# Stir-fried Tofu and Beansprouts with Noodles

This is a satisfying dish, which is both tasty and easy to make.

*Serves 4*

INGREDIENTS

225 g/8 oz firm tofu
groundnut oil, for deep frying
175 g/6 oz medium egg noodles
15 ml/1 tbsp sesame oil
5 ml/1 tsp cornflour
10 ml/2 tsp dark soy sauce
30 ml/1 tbsp Chinese rice wine
5 ml/1 tsp sugar
6–8 spring onions, cut diagonally
  into 2.5 cm/1 in lengths
3 garlic cloves, sliced
1 fresh green chilli, seeded
  and sliced
115 g/4 oz Chinese cabbage
  leaves, coarsely shredded
50 g/2 oz beansprouts
50 g/2 oz cashew nuts, toasted

*spring onion*

*garlic*

*sesame oil*

*Chinese cabbage*

*tofu*

*noodles*

*beansprouts*

*dark soy sauce*

*Chinese rice wine*

*green chilli*

**1** Drain the tofu and pat dry with kitchen paper. Cut the tofu into 2.5 cm/1 in cubes. Half-fill a wok with groundnut oil and heat to 180°C/350°F. Deep-fry the tofu in batches for 1–2 minutes until golden and crisp. Drain on kitchen paper. Carefully pour all but 30 ml/2 tbsp of the oil from the wok.

**2** Cook the noodles. Rinse them thoroughly under cold water and drain well. Toss in 10 ml/2 tsp of the sesame oil and set aside. In a bowl, blend together the cornflour, soy sauce, rice wine, sugar and remaining sesame oil.

**3** Reheat the 30 ml/2 tbsp of groundnut oil and, when hot, add the spring onions, garlic, chilli, Chinese cabbage and beansprouts. Stir-fry for 1–2 minutes.

**4** Add the tofu with the noodles and sauce. Cook, stirring, for about 1 minute until well mixed. Sprinkle over the cashew nuts. Serve at once.

# Cellophane Noodles with Pork

Unlike other types of noodle, cellophane noodles can be successfully reheated.

## Serves 3-4

INGREDIENTS
115 g/4 oz cellophane noodles
4 dried Chinese black mushrooms
225 g/8 oz boneless lean pork
30 ml/2 tbsp dark soy sauce
30 ml/2 tbsp Chinese rice wine
2 garlic cloves, crushed
15 ml/1 tbsp grated fresh
   root ginger
5 ml/1 tsp chilli oil
45 ml/3 tbsp groundnut oil
4-6 spring onions, chopped
5 ml/1 tsp cornflour blended
   with 175 ml/6 fl oz/¾ cup
   chicken stock or water
30 ml/2 tbsp chopped
   fresh coriander
salt and ground black pepper
coriander sprigs, to garnish

spring onions

noodles

chicken stock

Chinese rice wine

mushrooms

dark soy sauce

pork

chilli oil

groundnut oil

**1** Put the noodles and mushrooms in separate bowls and pour over warm water to cover. Leave to soak for 15–20 minutes until soft; drain well. Cut the noodles into 12.5 cm/5 in lengths using scissors or a knife. Squeeze out any water from the mushrooms, discard the stems and then finely chop the caps.

**2** Meanwhile, cut the pork into very small cubes. Put into a bowl with the soy sauce, rice wine, garlic, ginger and chilli oil, then leave for about 15 minutes. Drain, reserving the marinade.

**3** Heat a wok until hot, add the oil and swirl it around. Add the pork and mushrooms and stir-fry for 3 minutes. Add the spring onions and stir-fry for 1 minute. Stir in the cornflour, marinade and seasoning. Cook for about 1 minute.

**4** Add the noodles and stir-fry for about 2 minutes until the noodles absorb most of the liquid and the pork is cooked through. Stir in the chopped coriander. Taste and adjust the seasoning. Serve garnished with coriander sprigs.

# Spicy Fried Rice Sticks with Prawns

This recipe is based on the classic Thai noodle dish called *Pad Thai*. Popular all over Thailand, it is enjoyed morning, noon and night.

## VARIATION

For a vegetarian dish omit the dried shrimps and replace the king prawns with cubes of deep-fried tofu.

## Serves 4

INGREDIENTS

15 g/½ oz dried shrimps
15 ml/1 tbsp tamarind pulp
45 ml/3 tbsp Thai fish sauce (*nam pla*)
15 ml/1 tbsp sugar
2 garlic cloves, chopped
2 fresh red chillies, seeded and chopped
45 ml/3 tbsp groundnut oil
2 eggs, beaten
225 g/8 oz dried rice sticks, soaked in warm water for 30 minutes, refreshed under cold running water and drained
225 g/8 oz cooked peeled king prawns
3 spring onions, cut into 2.5 cm/1 in lengths
75 g/3 oz beansprouts
30 ml/2 tbsp roughly chopped roasted unsalted peanuts
30 ml/2 tbsp chopped fresh coriander
lime slices, to garnish

**1** Put the dried shrimps in a small bowl and pour over enough warm water to cover. Leave to soak for 30 minutes until soft; drain.

**2** Put the tamarind pulp in a bowl with 60 ml/4 tbsp hot water. Blend together, then press through a sieve to extract 30 ml/2 tbsp thick tamarind water. Mix the tamarind water with the fish sauce and sugar.

**3** Using a mortar and pestle, pound the garlic and chillies to form a paste. Heat a wok over a medium heat, add 15 ml/1 tbsp of the oil, then add the beaten eggs and stir for 1–2 minutes until the eggs are scrambled. Remove and set aside. Wipe the wok clean.

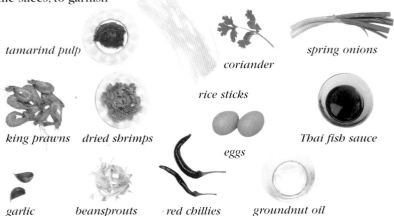

*tamarind pulp*

*coriander*

*spring onions*

*rice sticks*

*king prawns*   *dried shrimps*

*eggs*

*Thai fish sauce*

*garlic*   *beansprouts*   *red chillies*   *groundnut oil*

**4** Reheat the wok until hot, add the remaining oil, then the chilli paste and dried shrimps and stir-fry for 1 minute. Add the rice sticks and tamarind mixture and stir-fry for 3–4 minutes.

**5** Add the scrambled eggs, prawns, spring onions, beansprouts, peanuts and coriander, then stir-fry for 2 minutes until well mixed. Serve at once, garnishing each portion with lime slices.

# Indonesian Fried Rice

This fried rice dish makes an ideal supper on its own or as an accompaniment.

*Serves 4-6*

INGREDIENTS
4 shallots, roughly chopped
1 fresh red chilli, seeded
    and chopped
1 garlic clove, chopped
thin sliver of dried shrimp paste
45 ml/3 tbsp vegetable oil
225 g/8 oz boneless lean pork,
    cut into fine strips
175 g/6 oz/1¼ cups long grain
    white rice, boiled and cooled
3-4 spring onions, thinly sliced
115 g/4 oz cooked peeled prawns
30 ml/2 tbsp sweet soy sauce
    (*kecap manis*)
chopped fresh coriander and
    fine cucumber shreds, to
    garnish

*spring onions*

*prawns*

*vegetable oil*

*pork*

*chilli*

*rice*

*shallots*

*soy sauce*

*dried shrimp paste*

*garlic*

**1** In a mortar pound the shallots, chilli, garlic and shrimp paste with a pestle until they form a paste.

**2** Heat a wok until hot, add 30 ml/ 2 tbsp of the oil and swirl it around. Add the pork and stir-fry for 2–3 minutes. Remove the pork from the wok, set aside and keep warm.

**3** Add the remaining oil to the wok. When hot, add the spiced shallot paste and stir-fry for about 30 seconds.

**4** Reduce the heat. Add the rice, spring onions and prawns. Stir-fry for 2–3 minutes. Add the pork and sprinkle over the soy sauce. Stir-fry for 1 minute. Serve garnished with the chopped coriander and cucumber shreds.

# Fried Rice with Spices

This dish is mildly spiced, suitable as an accompaniment to any curried dish. The whole spices are not meant to be eaten.

*Serves 3-4*

INGREDIENTS
175 g/6 oz/1¼ cups basmati rice
2.5 ml/½ tsp salt
15 ml/1 tbsp ghee or butter
8 whole cloves
4 green cardamom pods, bruised
1 bay leaf
7.5 cm/3 in cinnamon stick
5 ml/1 tsp black peppercorns
5 ml/1 tsp cumin seeds
5 ml/1 tsp coriander seeds

*rice*

*ghee*          *coriander*

*bay leaf*

*cinnamon stick*

*cumin*

*cardamom*

*cloves*

## VARIATION
You could add 2.5 ml/½ tsp ground turmeric to the rice in step 2 to colour it yellow.

**1** Put the rice in a colander and wash under cold running water until the water clears. Put in a bowl and pour 600 ml/1 pint/2½ cups fresh water over the rice. Leave the rice to soak for 30 minutes; then drain thoroughly.

**2** Put the rice, salt and 600ml/1 pint/2½ cups water in a heavy-based pan. Bring to the boil, then simmer, covered, for about 10 minutes. The rice should be just cooked with still a little bite to it. Drain off any excess water, fluff up the grains with a fork, then spread it out on a tray and leave to cool.

**3** Heat the ghee or butter in a karahi or wok until foaming, add the spices and stir-fry for 1 minute.

**4** Add the cooled rice and stir-fry for 3–4 minutes until warmed through. Serve at once.

# Thai Fried Rice

This hot and spicy dish is easy to prepare and makes a meal in itself.

## Serves 4

INGREDIENTS
225 g/8 oz Thai jasmine rice
45 ml/3 tbsp vegetable oil
1 onion, chopped
1 small red pepper, seeded and
    cut into 2 cm/¾ in cubes
350 g/12 oz skinless and boneless
    chicken breasts, cut into 2 cm/
    ¾ in cubes
1 garlic clove, crushed
15 ml/1 tbsp mild curry paste
2.5 ml/½ tsp paprika
2.5 ml/½ tsp ground turmeric
30 ml/2 tbsp Thai fish sauce
    (nam pla)
2 eggs, beaten
salt and ground black pepper
fried basil leaves, to garnish

rice

Thai fish sauce

chicken

curry paste

onion

egg

red pepper

paprika

turmeric

vegetable oil

## VARIATION
Add 50 g/2 oz frozen peas to the chicken in step 3, if you wish.

**1** Put the rice in a sieve and wash well under cold running water. Put the rice in a heavy-based pan with 1.5 litres/2½ pints/6¼ cups boiling water. Return to the boil, then simmer, uncovered, for 8–10 minutes; drain well. Spread out the grains on a tray and leave to cool.

**2** Heat a wok until hot, add 30ml/ 2 tbsp of the oil and swirl it around. Add the onion and red pepper and stir-fry for 1 minute.

**3** Add the chicken, garlic, curry paste and spices and stir-fry for 2–3 minutes.

**4** Reduce the heat to medium, add the cooled rice, fish sauce and seasoning. Stir-fry for 2–3 minutes until the rice is very hot.

**5** Make a well in the centre of the rice and add the remaining oil. When hot, add the beaten eggs, leave to cook for about 2 minutes until lightly set, then stir into the rice.

**6** Scatter over the fried basil leaves and serve at once.

# Stir-fried Noodles with Sweet Soy Salmon

Teriyaki sauce forms the marinade for the salmon in this recipe. Served with soft-fried noodles, it makes a stunning dish.

COOK'S TIP
It is important to scrape the marinade off the fish as any remaining pieces of ginger or garlic would burn during grilling and spoil the finished dish.

## Serves 4

INGREDIENTS
350 g/12 oz salmon fillet
30 ml/2 tbsp Japanese soy sauce (*shoyu*)
30 ml/2 tbsp sake
60 ml/4 tbsp mirin or sweet sherry
5 ml/1 tsp light brown soft sugar
10 ml/2 tsp grated fresh root ginger
3 garlic cloves, 1 crushed, and 2 sliced into rounds
30 ml/2 tbsp groundnut oil
225 g/8 oz dried egg noodles, cooked and drained
50 g/2 oz alfalfa sprouts
30 ml/2 tbsp sesame seeds, lightly toasted

garlic
sesame seeds
noodles
alfalfa sprouts
sake
mirin
sugar
salmon
Japanese soy sauce
groundnut oil
ginger

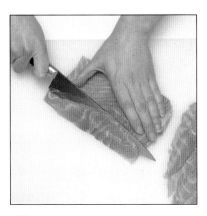

**1** Thinly slice the salmon, then place in a shallow dish.

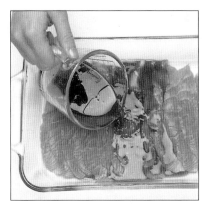

**2** In a bowl, mix together the soy sauce, sake, mirin or sherry, sugar, ginger and crushed garlic. Pour over the salmon, cover and leave for 30 minutes.

**3** Preheat the grill. Drain the salmon, scraping off and reserving the marinade. Place the salmon in a single layer on a baking sheet. Cook under the grill for 2–3 minutes without turning.

**4** Meanwhile, heat a wok until hot, add the oil and swirl it around. Add the garlic rounds and cook until golden brown but not burnt.

**5** Add the cooked noodles and reserved marinade to the wok and stir-fry for 3–4 minutes until the marinade has reduced slightly to a syrupy glaze and coats the noodles.

**6** Toss in the alfalfa sprouts, then remove immediately from the heat. Transfer to warmed serving plates and top with the salmon. Sprinkle over the toasted sesame seeds. Serve at once.

# Singapore Noodles

A delicious supper dish with a stunning mix of flavours and textures.

## Serves 4

INGREDIENTS

225 g/8 oz dried egg noodles
45 ml/3 tbsp groundnut oil
1 onion, chopped
2.5 cm/1 in piece fresh root
    ginger, finely chopped
1 garlic clove, finely chopped
15 ml/1 tbsp Madras
    curry powder
2.5 ml/½ tsp salt
115 g/4 oz cooked chicken or
    pork, finely shredded
115 g/4 oz cooked peeled prawns
115 g/4 oz Chinese cabbage
    leaves, shredded
115 g/4 oz beansprouts
60 ml/4 tbsp chicken stock
15–30 ml/1–2 tbsp dark soy sauce
1–2 fresh red chillies, seeded
    and finely shredded
4 spring onions, finely shredded

beansprouts

noodles

Chinese cabbage

ginger

curry powder

chicken

dark soy sauce

onion

stock

red chillies

spring onions

groundnut oil

prawns

**1** Cook the noodles according to the packet instructions. Rinse thoroughly under cold water and drain well. Toss in 15 ml/1 tbsp of the oil and set aside.

**2** Heat a wok until hot, add the remaining oil and swirl it around. Add the onion, ginger and garlic and stir-fry for about 2 minutes.

**3** Add the curry powder and salt, stir-fry for 30 seconds, then add the egg noodles, chicken or pork and prawns. Stir-fry for 3–4 minutes.

**4** Add the Chinese cabbage and beansprouts and stir-fry for 1–2 minutes. Sprinkle in the stock and soy sauce to taste and toss well until evenly mixed. Serve at once, garnished with the shredded red chillies and spring onions.

# Noodles with Ginger and Coriander

Here is a simple noodle dish that goes well with most oriental dishes. It can also be served as a snack for 2-3 people.

*Serves 4-6*

INGREDIENTS
handful of fresh coriander sprigs
225 g/8 oz dried egg noodles
45 ml/3 tbsp groundnut oil
5 cm/2 in piece fresh root ginger, cut into fine shreds
6-8 spring onions, cut into shreds
30 ml/2 tbsp light soy sauce
salt and ground black pepper

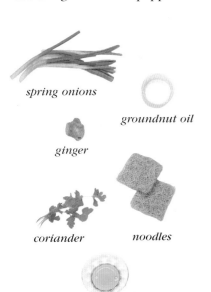

*spring onions*

*groundnut oil*

*ginger*

*coriander*　　*noodles*

*light soy sauce*

## COOK'S TIP
Many of the dried egg noodles available are sold packed in layers. As a guide allow 1 layer of noodles per person as an average portion for a main dish.

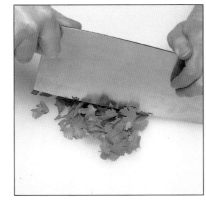

**1** Strip the leaves from the coriander stalks. Pile them on a chopping board and coarsely chop them using a cleaver or large sharp knife.

**2** Cook the noodles according to the packet instructions. Rinse under cold water and drain well. Toss in 15 ml/ 1 tbsp of the oil.

**3** Heat a wok until hot, add the remaining oil and swirl it around. Add the ginger and stir-fry for a few seconds, then add the noodles and spring onions. Stir-fry for 3–4 minutes until hot.

**4** Sprinkle over the soy sauce, coriander and seasoning. Toss well, then serve at once.

# INDEX

**A**

Aubergines:
Szechuan aubergines, 70

**B**

Beansprouts:
preparing, 15
stir-fried tofu and beansprouts
with noodles, 84
Beef:
beef rendang, 52
chilli beef with basil, 55

**C**

Cauliflower:
Balti potatoes and
cauliflower, 77
Chick peas:
spicy chick peas with
ginger, 80
Chicken:
Balti chicken tikka masala, 62
glazed chicken with cashew
nuts, 58
stock, 19
sweetcorn and chicken soup,
33.
Thai red chicken curry, 60
Chillies, 8
flowers, 17
removing seeds from, 16
Coconut:
fresh coconut milk, 19
spiced coconut mushrooms,
76
spiced prawns with coconut,
51
Crab:
hot spicy crab claws, 32
Cucumber fan, 17

**D**

Deep-frying, 20

**Duck:**
sweet-sour duck with mango,
66

**E**

Eggs:
stir-fried vegetables with
coriander omelette, 68
Equipment, 12

**F**

Fish:
fish balls with Chinese
greens, 40
green seafood curry, 46
spicy battered fish, 39
sweet-and-sour fish, 44
Thai fish cakes, 25
Thai seafood salad, 38

**G**

Garam masala, 19
Garlic, peeling and chopping,
16
Ginger, peeling and chopping,
16

**H**

Herbs, 8, 9
chopping, 15

**K**

Kaffir lime leaves, preparing, 15

**L**

Lamb:
lettuce-wrapped garlic lamb,
22
paper-thin lamb with spring
onions, 54
spiced lamb with spinach, 57
Lemon grass, peeling and
chopping, 15
Lettuce-wrapped garlic lamb, 22

**M**

Meat, preparing, 14
Mushrooms:
red-cooked tofu with Chinese
mushrooms, 78
spiced coconut mushrooms, 76
Mussels:
lemon-grass-and-basil-scented
mussels, 50

**N**

Noodles:
cellophane noodles with
pork, 85
crispy noodles with mixed
vegetables, 82
noodles with ginger and
coriander, 95
Singapore noodles, 94
spicy fried noodles with
prawns, 86
stir-fried noodles with sweet
soy salmon, 92
stir-fried tofu and beansprouts
with noodles, 84

**P**

Pak choi:
Chinese greens with oyster
sauce, 71
fish balls with Chinese
greens, 40
Pork:
cellophane noodles with
pork, 85
Chinese spiced salt spareribs,
26
lemon grass pork, 56
steamed spiced pork and
water chestnut wontons, 28
Potatoes:
Spicy potatoes and
cauliflower, 77

**Prawns:**
green seafood curry, 46
quick-fried prawns with hot
spices, 36
spiced prawns with coconut,
51
spicy fried noodles with
prawns, 86
Thai seafood salad, 38

**R**

Red snapper with ginger and
spring onions, 42
Rice:
Fried rice with spices, 89
Indonesian fried rice, 88
Thai fried rice, 90

**S**

Salmon:
stir-fried noodles with sweet
soy salmon, 92
Sauces, 8, 9
preparing, 14
Scallops:
spiced scallops in their shells,
49
Thai seafood salad, 38
Spices, 8, 9
Spinach:
spiced lamb with spinach, 57
stir-fried spinach with garlic
and sesame seeds, 73
Spring greens:
crispy seaweed with flaked
almonds, 24
Spring onions:
paper-thin lamb with spring
onions, 54
red snapper with ginger and
spring onions, 42
spring onion brush, 17
Spring rolls:

crispy spring rolls with sweet
chilli dipping sauce, 34
Squid:
green seafood curry, 46
squid with peppers in a black
bean sauce, 48
Thai seafood salad, 38
Steaming, 21
Stir-frying, 20
Storecupboard ingredient, 10
Sweetcorn and chicken soup,
33

**T**

Thai green curry paste, 18
Thai red curry paste, 18
Tofu:
red-cooked tofu with Chinese
mushrooms, 78
stir-fried tofu and beansprouts
with noodles, 84
Turkey:
stir-fried turkey with broccoli
and shiitake mushrooms, 64

**V**

Vegetables, 10
crispy noodles with mixed
vegetables, 82
deep-fried root vegetables with
spiced salt, 72
preparing, 14
stir-fried vegetables with
coriander omelette, 68
vegetable tempura, 30

**Y**

yellow flower vegetables, 74

**W**

Water chestnuts:
steamed spiced pork and
water chestnut wontons, 28

96